P9-BYV-868

THE MAKING
OF CHAMPIONS

THE MAKING OF CHAMPIONS

Soviet Sports for Children and Teenagers

Miriam Morton

Atheneum 1974 New York

To the world's
youngest sports lovers

Acknowledgment

The largest number of the photographs was made available by the Novosti Press Agency; the rest by the various children's sports schools and organizations. The author is most grateful.

Contents

THE MAKING
OF CHAMPIONS

A cyclist team training at the Sports Section of a state farm (kolkhoz) *near Moscow.*

1

A Nation of
Sports Lovers

IN THE SOVIET UNION CHILDREN ARE ENCOURAGED EARLY to start thinking about their life goals. Discussion of their future goes on nearly all the time. At Moscow School No. 130, for instance, the boys and girls were asked to suppose that by some magic they could achieve anything they wanted to. They were asked to write down what they would choose to do. One of the boys, Sasha (Sandy) Bondarsky, twelve years old, wrote this answer: "I would arrange for all of us to get the best grades in school. Then I want to be a good footballer. My friends and I would play on the world team and fly to other planets to take on the Martians and the rest."

A number of the other answers revealed equally grand ambitions for a glorious future in sports.

Such reactions are not a coincidence, for Soviet children

are part of a nation of sports enthusiasts. Most of them are not just fans but are active in one or more of the many popular sports.

The statistics tell an amazing story:

In 1960, there were 186,000 active sports groups and sports centers—societies, clubs, recreation centers, and sports schools. By 1968, the number had grown to 208,000. At the same time, the sizes of the groups had also grown enormously. The 186,000 groups had a total membership of 28 million; the 208,000, a membership of 54 million. The figure for 1971 was 65 million—one out of every four persons was involved in sports.

Of these 65 million, 40 million had won the all-around athletic pin. It carries the initials GTO. The letters stand for the Russian words meaning "physically fit for work and self-defense." Actually, however, this pin is generally awarded to those who attain the physical fitness needed for training in sports. The pin is earned only after the individual passes a number of athletic tests.

There are still other statistics to show how rapidly the popularity of sports has grown in the USSR. In 1960 there were 20,600 Masters of Sports. This, except for the rarely bestowed Honored Master of Sports rank given to world champions, is the highest rank. By 1968 there were more than three times as many Masters of Sports—70,000. The increase occurred without any lowering of standards. To become a Master, the athlete must first pass tests for three lower ratings. Each rating is based on tests and on proved achievement in a chosen sport. Children of twelve may become Masters of Sports, if they meet the requirements.

The Palace of Pioneers in Tashkent, Uzbekistan, accommodating the children's Sports Section where volleyball, swimming, basketball, soccer and chess are taught.

A training session at a sports school for boxing in Soviet Armenia.

Soccer practice at a sports school on the Black Sea coast.

As for sports facilities, in 1960 there were 1,977 stadiums seating 1,500 or more spectators; in 1968 there were 3,065. Each such stadium has with it a group of buildings accommodating gymnasiums, swimming pools, dressing rooms, coaches' quarters, and so forth.

The number of football (soccer) fields in 1960, was 32,800; in 1968, 91,900. In the same 8-year period the number of volleyball, basketball, and tennis courts increased from 259,600 to 419,000. By 1968 there were 37,900 indoor gymnasiums and 34,300 sports fields usable for a variety of games, and the increase since then has been proportionate. These fields and courts do not include the ones on the premises of regular schools.

Many of these facilities exist just for the use of boys and girls, and some of the rest are open to their use. In 1972 there were some 20 million children and teenagers who belonged to special sports groups. Among these, 7 million had won the rating of "Young Sportsman"—a special designation for the more than average young athlete. The very best go on to try for the four ratings for adult sportsmen and sportswomen: Ratings 3, 2, 1 and Master of Sports—in that order.

The Soviet Union as a nation developed during a period of growing worldwide interest in sports. But there are other reasons for the unusual enthusiasm for, and participation in, sports in the country, and for their lavish support by the Government. From the very beginning, the Union of Soviet Socialist Republics has had national leaders who felt that sports were a necessary means for developing a physically fit, mentally alert, competitive, and achieving nation. They also saw in a broad national sports program a means for developing, both in the young and adult citizen, physical endurance for self-defense in case of invasion and war.

Participating in sports also encourages loyalty through the stimulus of competition—loyalty to one's team, town, village, native republic, or country.

Lenin, the first leader of the Soviet state, set an example. He proclaimed the importance of sports and even participated himself. He bicycled daily and hiked as often as time permitted. To exercise his mind, he played chess—which, in Russia, is considered a sport because it calls for skill, practice, and a strong competitive attitude. Under Lenin's leadership, physical education was introduced in the school system in a matter of months after the founding of the Soviet state, in 1918.

In the years since, the goals originally set for a nationwide sports program have not changed, nor have the means of paying for it. Sports share in the public health budget and in the overall education budget. They are also partly supported by trade and professional unions and other organizations with immense memberships, including the army. The sports-sponsoring organizations set aside large amounts of money from their membership dues for the purpose. Sports are publicly financed because the theory is: "Every ruble invested in sports is really an investment in health, character building, and patriotism."

No matter how sports programs are financed—from the public health budget, the budget for education, or by the mass organizations—it is the Ministry of Education, through its Committee on Physical Fitness, that sets the curriculum and standards of achievement. It also specifies the qualifications of the coaches, and the nature and frequency of medical checkups for trainees.

Participation in sports by children or adults is entirely voluntary. For the young there is one exception: schoolchildren from seven to seventeen years of age have to take physical education classes two hours each week in their regular schools.

Surprisingly, in the Soviet Union where academic learning is stressed so much, little distinction is made between a strong interest in sports and in the three major fields of study—science, mathematics, and literature. Furthermore, it is generally believed that without some sports activity for fun, for a change of pace and release of tension, the serious student will not succeed well.

The father of thirteen-year-old Fedya (Teddy) put it this way: "I hope my son will some day be a writer—it is what he has chosen to become. He has already written some fine stories. But I have been urging him not to give up wrestling. I also told him that he must get only four A's in school —in literature, history, conduct, and *physical education.* In literature, because without knowing how to read and understand a good book, he will not grow up to understand and love his fellowman. Without a good knowledge of his country's history, he will not know his own homeland and how he can contribute to its welfare. If he doesn't learn to conduct himself as he should, he will not be respected. And *without sports,* he will not have the physical and mental stamina to achieve his main goal, that of becoming a good writer."

A gymnasium in a Sports Section in a children's recreational center in Tashkent, Uzbekistan.

The head coach of a school for acrobatic gymnastics explained why Tanya, a slow learner at her regular school, was not dropped from the gymnastics group in order that she might have more time for schoolwork: "She loves acrobatics, works hard at it and has made fine progress. She would be heartbroken if she were dropped. We had several talks with her, and she will try harder to improve her school grades by organizing her time better. One of the older girl gymnasts is helping Tanya improve her grades by tutoring her regularly."

Teachers, coaches, many parents, and the schoolchildren themselves believe that one can do well both in school and in sports.

The looked-for reward for the many years of hard work that go into becoming a district, city, regional, or interna-

9

tional champion is not money, but honor and admiration. In the Soviet Union all sports are amateur. They are amateur in the sense that there are no privately owned teams, and that no sportsman or sportswoman can "turn professional" and earn a salary or fee.

Fine Soviet athletes may earn a living by serving as coaches after earning a college degree in a physical culture institute, with a major in their sport. Alexander Medved, three-time gold medal Olympic champion in Greco-Roman heavyweight wrestling, earns his living as a physical education instructor. But others work in other fields. Elena Petushkova, the world champion in dressage, is a remarkable horsewoman and also a successful scholar. She holds a professorship in biology at Moscow University. Sergei Belov, star basketball player on the 1972 Olympic team, is a student at the Shipbuilding Institute of Leningrad. He lives on the stipend that is given to all college students who maintain good grades.

The best athletes receive nonmaterial awards in addition to their trophies, prizes, and medals. They are lavished with public admiration and praise. They become local or national heroes. They are honored in a variety of ways: six of the 1972 Olympic medalists received the highest national honor—the Order of Lenin. Among them were Alexander Medved, the wrestler; Vasili Alexeyev, the super-heavyweight lifter; Sergei Belov, the basketball star; and Valeri Bortzov, sprinter.

Since 1968, a number of young men and women have been given an award called "Brilliance in Sports," for their "extraordinary daring and will to win." Nona Gaprindash-

Three-time Olympic champion heavyweight wrestler, Alexander Medved, with his American rival, Charles Taylor, at the games.

Alexander Belov, star of the winning basketball team at the 1972 summer Olympics.

Valeri Borzov, best sprinter in the 1972 summer Olympics, holding up his gold medals for his 100- and 200-meter runs.

vili, the Soviet woman world chess champion, was one of these.

The names of great athletes are entered in the honor books of youth organizations, next to the names of outstanding cosmonauts, scientists, poets, and war heroes. Fifteen hundred Masters of Sports have been further honored with the rank of Honored Master of Sports. None of these awards and honors carries a prize of money.

To attract millions of children and teenagers to sports, sports training and events are made interesting and exciting. The Russians seem to have a gift for giving everything they do a theatrical flair. They spare no effort in staging colorful sports parades, pageants and festivals. A number of sports have their own songs. The Soviet ways of popularizing sports are often genuinely original, spectacular, and a lot of fun.

Children are drawn into the world of sports at a very early age. Recently, in a suburb of the Siberian city of Novosibirsk, 110 five- and six-year-olds took part in an unusual sports "meet" in the local stadium. The children were from eleven kindergartens, and they competed in a variety of "events": physical exercises, 2-meter running, 50-meter tricycle races, and very mini-soccer. Novosibirsk is a city the whole country watches. It is new, experimental, and inhabited by very gifted young scientists and educators and their families. With their sports "event" for kindergartners reported in the national papers, thousands of other communities may soon start their own sports programs for pre-schoolers.

August 12 has been proclaimed National Physical Cul-

Preschoolers in Novosibirsk take part in a mini-mini-tournament.

ture Day. The millions of children and teenagers in the numerous ordinary and *sports* summer camps celebrate the day with final meets. Record-achieving young athletes are awarded pins, indicating their new sports rating. Winning teams, their sunburned faces beaming, come forward to receive their prizes, with trumpets blaring and fans singing, shouting, and clapping. The festivities are marked by exhibition games and feats. No doubt, many a camper returns to everyday life with a newly kindled hope that someday he or she may win not a camp contest but an Olympic contest.

One of the Russian traditions in sports is for a team to free a flock of homing pigeons whenever they win, to let

13

their entire region know the happy news. "Thus far, however," writes a Soviet sports journalist, "no one has suggested what to release when the other team wins." He assures his readers that the matter is still being studied.

Radio and television programs for youngsters conduct interesting sports classes. For instance, the daily, early-morning radio program for Pioneer age children—there are 29 million of them—devotes an entire broadcast to sports once a week. (The Pioneer organization is for children eleven to fifteen years of age, and is in a number of ways similar to the Boy Scout and Girl Scout movement in the United States. It sets high goals for achievement and patriotism. Both boys and girls belong to its thousands of clubs.) The Pioneer radio program features interviews with sports heroes, sports songs, and sports poetry. It also answers questions from children about how to make do-it-yourself sports equipment and how to budget time so as to have enough for school-work and for sports.

Junior international competitions are given a lot of publicity in the children's press. They fire the ambitions and competitive spirit of young sports lovers, and generate much excitement among them. Soviet children and teen-agers take part in the Junior Olympics held in Europe every four years, with as many as 3,000 participants from 70 countries. Contests are held in the ten traditional events: track and field, gymnastics, swimming, water polo, boys and girls volleyball, fencing, basketball, and tennis. The Junior Olympics are also known as *Universiadas*. Because of their good training and experience in competitions, Soviet youngsters make a very good showing at the *Universiadas*. The many newspapers and magazines for young readers report interestingly and in great detail on this important sports event.

One of the most inspiring and eye-filling events glorifying and glamorizing sports is the *USSR People's Games.* The Lenin Central Stadium lies in a park on the elevated southwest end of Moscow. Since 1956, the huge sports center has been the site of this national event, which culminates in the final selection of Olympic contestants. The People's Games are staged every fourth year—the year before the World Olympics. This is now a tradition. The purpose is to involve as many people as possible in physical culture and sports and to discover new athletes of international caliber.

Besides leading to the final screening of Olympic contestants, the many levels of competition help select teenage athletes for more intensive training. The People's Games feature: basketball, boxing, freestyle and Greco-Roman wrestling, cycling, water polo, volleyball, gymnastics, rowing, equestrian sports, track and field, ·swimming, diving, shooting, archery, the modern pentathlon, tennis, weight lifting, fencing, soccer, motorcycle racing, table tennis, and chess. People come from all fifteen Soviet republics to compete.

Before the contests begin, the thousands of athletes parade through the Red Square. So many participate that the parade lasts several hours. The marchers, including many children's teams, are dressed in festive sports attire and carry a forest of banners. It is an exciting event for young and old. And it makes children eager to learn and compete,

Children's sports teams in the People's Games Parade on Red Square in Moscow.

so they too may be a part of the Games someday.

The Russians are also irresistibly challenged by the greatness of American athletes. Coaches, physical education experts, and journalists have kept in close touch with American sports. They have also studied closely our methods of training. In fact they have been so influenced by contact with the American sports world that they have included many of our terms in their own language. They constantly use the words *start, penalty, goal, ring, finish, crawl, pass, time, court, tennis, round, match, sportsman, trainer, football.* There are no Russian equivalents for these terms. Of course, they spell the English words with Russian letters. English sports have also contributed to this vocabulary.

The Soviet sports vocabulary has not, however, adopted the word "fan." For this the Russians have their very own word. It is *"bolel'schik,"* derived from the word *bol'—*

Bolel'schiki (fans) *watching a sports event on the island of Sakhalin in the Soviet Pacific northwest.*

meaning "pain." A bolel'schik is thus a person who *feels* for, who "hurts" for the athlete as he experiences the pain of exhausting effort or the pain of losing. Perhaps this word, which they use instead of an equivalent for "fan," proves best how seriously and emotionally they take their sports. Before the 1972 Olympics, a sports leader said: "All of us will, of course, be very anxious, we'll *hurt* for our countrymen athletes. And particularly will we *hurt* for those who will carry our country's banner at the Games for the first time."

Although Soviet sports leaders have had their eyes fixed on American sports and sports of other nations, there are those who have also been inventing Soviet variations of old sports. "Sambo," for instance, is a combination of the best holds used in every variety of wrestling, including the special forms of wrestling used by different ethnic Soviet peoples. The letters that make up the word "sambo" are the first letters of the Russian words meaning "self-defense without weapons." In other words, it is a form of wrestling that can also be used against an unarmed attacker.

Soviet boys love sambo and are being trained in it on an increasingly larger scale. It is something they can all learn, large or small, because the weight of the opponents is taken into consideration when there is a draw; the one weighing less is declared the winner. Sambo is something like judo but is different enough to be considered a separate form of wrestling. Its popularity is growing in several other European countries, and it has also been taken up in Japan. The Japanese became interested when one of their world champions in judo was defeated by a Soviet "samboist" in 20

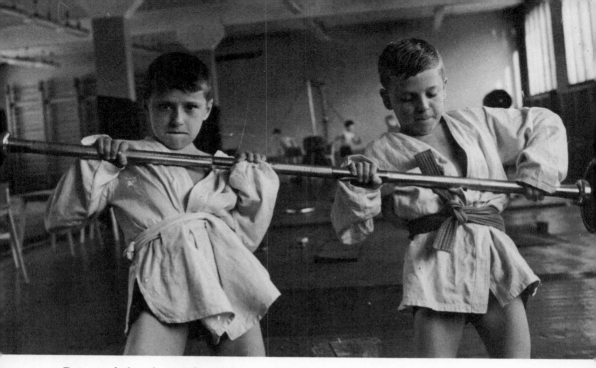

Boys training in sambo, doing weightlifting to strengthen muscles.

Boys training in sambo, a Russian form of judo, strengthening their arm muscles.

Two young samboists practicing the art.

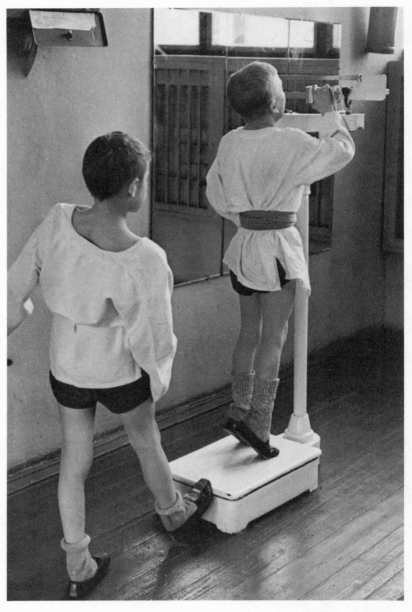

Weighing-in before a training session in sambo. The trick (foot on scale) is international.

seconds before an audience of 10,000 in Tokyo. This happened before sambo became a separate sport.

Not everyone in the Soviet Union approves of sambo as a sport for children. Some consider it too violent because the only way to win over an opponent is by causing him pain. (Several of the sports school directors and coaches with whom the author talked were so negative about sambo that they were even reluctant to discuss it.)

Although the Soviet athletes and their leaders are so anxious to stand out as the world's best, they seem to hold to a fine sense of good sportsmanship. For instance, they constantly use the slogan, "May the best man win." Losing is not regarded as a disgrace by any means.

They are always ready to praise American sports stars. After seeing our great little young gymnast, Kathy Rigby, perform at an international tournament in Riga, Soviet Latvia, the then Russian world champion gymnast, Larissa Latynina, said: "Kathy Rigby is a splendid gymnast, confident in all the exercises and simply matchless on the beam, which everyone regards as the trickiest piece of apparatus. Kathy is unquestionably the ace of the American team. My first acquaintance with American women gymnasts was in 1961, when our national team toured the United States. It is a pleasure to see how much progress the Americans have made in this sport since then."

The American gymnast, John Cosby, is also a favorite with Russian athletes, and they often sing his praises.

The director of a Leningrad swimming school for children and teens expressed great admiration for American swimmers during the author's visit to his school. He wanted to know by what magic the United States produced so many world record breakers. He expressed the universal Soviet determination to spot young athletes early and develop ways of helping them become world champions.

Unlike those in America, Soviet colleges and universities do not produce topnotch sports people. (Nor do the secondary schools concentrate on sports.) Sports are not taken seriously on Soviet campuses. The students may play against each other informally, but there is no tradition of intercollegiate rivalry. Students take part in sports mainly for fun and exercise. Soccer, volleyball, and basketball are the most popular. Baseball has only recently gained in popularity. (It is the Cubans studying in Russia who have introduced it.) The smacking sound of bat against ball can now be heard out there in Moscow University. But instead of the colleges, it is mainly the factory, collective farm, and union sports societies and clubs that turn up the most promising athletes.

Another major source of potential championship material are the several thousand special *Sports Schools for Children and Teenagers.* In 1971 there were 3,580 such schools.

To really understand the importance of sports in the Soviet Union, one must know something about all of the varied programs available for children.

2

The Sports Schools for Children and Teenagers (Diush's)

THE USSR HAS PIONEERED IN THE DEVELOPMENT OF WHAT they call the *Detskaia-Iunosheskaia Shkola* (*School for Children and Teenagers*)—the Russian abbreviation is "DIUSH." Soviet sportswriters like to refer to these schools, which are sports schools, as "schools without desks."

Such schools first began to open in the late 1950s. They were designed for boys and girls with a strong interest in a special sport and with good enough physical abilities to achieve some success. In 1966 there were about 800 DIUSH's. By 1971, that number had increased to 3,580. The enrollment by 1971 ran to several million. And leaders in sports education felt this was a mere beginning.

Why were sports schools established? How are they run? What sports do they teach? Who is eligible to train in them? Who decides on the program and the standards? Who pays for the buildings, equipment, and instruction?

The regular eight- and ten-year schools do not usually have adequate outdoor space or indoor facilities for an extended physical education and sports program. This is especially true of city schools. Nor is there room in the curriculum of the regular schools for the many hours that are required to train highly qualified young athletes. The curriculum is too loaded with academic subjects. The Soviet student has to take more classes in literature and foreign languages, in science and mathematics during his six-day school week than do students in most other countries. The regular schools therefore limit physical education to two hours a week. This curtailed program is well-run, but it merely helps maintain good physical fitness.

Yet much more athletic activity is deemed necessary in the USSR for the development of strong young bodies and minds, as well as to assure the country's good record in international sports. Also, thousands upon thousands of boys and girls love sports and want to excel in one, and many of them are willing to put in years of very hard work to compete for national and international championship, for the exhilaration and pleasure it brings.

The DIUSH's enroll students from eleven to eighteen years of age, sometimes even younger ones. Classes and practice periods are held in the afternoon and evening, and sometimes very early in the morning as well—before classes start at the regular school.

The schools, no matter what sport they specialize in, follow a specific program of instruction and training, using an official syllabus. Each syllabus states the following general reasons and aims for the schools:

A warming-up session at a children's sports school in Baku, Azerbaijan, a Soviet republic on the Caspian Sea.

25

Experience with the sports schools for children and teenagers has shown that, properly run, they will provide an excellent means of attracting children and teenagers to a *systematic* study of their chosen sport. They will provide the training of quality athletes as well as develop needed assistants for physical culture groups in the communities and in the regular school sports clubs. The curriculum must have a precise learning and training program directed by a highly qualified staff of coaches.

How best to achieve these aims, and to increase the role of the DIUSH in training athletes who could hold high the banner of Soviet sports internationally, was determined in 1970 by the Council of Ministers of the USSR, the Ministry of Education, and the Communist Party.

Together these top Government agencies drew up standard syllabuses, which specify that the sports schools are to develop all-around athletes to their *highest potential*, improve the physical fitness of the youngsters in their care and make them generally strong. In order to achieve these aims, the staff of each DIUSH is required to conduct a *year-round* schedule of training that will kindle in each student an ever stronger interest in his chosen sport and in achieving as much as he is capable of doing.

The young sports lovers are not only to have their muscles trained, but are to be given the moral ideals of the Soviet society, stressing the rules of good sportsmanship, good fellowship toward rivals, self-discipline, loyalty to the team. The sports students must also develop a strong "taste for victory." Competitions must be scheduled regularly to give the boys and girls an opportunity to develop these attitudes.

The DIUSH is also required to organize a parents' group and to make the parents at least partially responsible for the children's regular attendance.

In special circumstances—climate, the newness of a settlement or community, or the unavailability of certain equipment and facilities—a sports school may offer less than the prescribed program, but the basic goals must not be ignored.

Children and teenagers are free to choose their sport. They may switch to another sport if there is a better chance of succeeding in it. Any child who wants to attend a local sports school fills out a simple form. He takes home a second one on which his parents indicate their permission; and the principal of his regular school gives his opinion of the applicant's work and conduct. The child then has to pass a strict medical examination given by the

Medical checkup for a young sportsman.

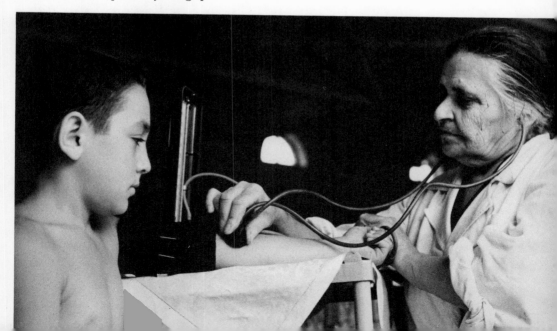

A young trainee in weightlifting and his coach.

school's (the DIUSH's) physician. (In the course of the year he will get two more medical checkups at the sports school.)

Generally, the applicant has to have a good record of grades and behavior at his regular school. Occasionally, however, a "difficult" boy or girl will be accepted in the hope that his or her interest in sports and the careful guidance the DIUSH gives will correct the wrong work habits or conduct.

At the beginning, every student has to spend from several months to a year and a half doing carefully selected exercises to toughen up for the strenuous training to come. He is also expected to swim, play basketball, and do a lot of running to increase his strength, quickness, and endurance. This he does under the supervision of a coach.

Once his actual training in a sport has begun, every student must take part in planned competitions. He is excused from regular school for out-of-town contests. The trips never exceed three or four days, and he has to make up the missed schoolwork.

The training program in the DIUSH starts with two-hour sessions three times a week for children from eleven to thirteen years of age, and progresses to as many as 5 weekly sessions, each lasting two to three hours for the oldest teenage students.

It is considered most practical for sports schools to teach one to four sports only. This means that large cities may have a number of schools. The city of Kiev, in the Ukraine, has seven sports schools. School No. 1 specializes in basketball, soccer, tennis, and Ping-Pong. The enrollment in these four divisions totals about 3,000. There are sixty coaches, most of whom hold degrees from physical education institutes and have a Master of Sports rating.

The sports school complex on the Lenin Hills in Moscow has schools for swimming, acrobatic gymnastics, chess, and volleyball for boys and girls; it also has an artistic gymnastics school only for girls. Together, these several sports schools, in addition to their regular program, sponsor special athletic activities at ten regular Moscow schools. They help with training, meets, sports parades, and with singling out promising young athletes for training at a DIUSH.

With a few exceptions, the sports schools specialize in the sports in which the Soviet world teams have made their best showing: basketball, soccer, water polo, chess, equestrian events, track and field, weight lifting, speed skating, figure skating, skiing, hockey, gymnastics, fencing, wrestling, boxing, rowing. In all of these sports the students are trained in accordance with international forms and rules, so that they may later be able to compete in European or other foreign events.

Although the USSR has not been outstanding in swimming competitions, a tremendous effort is being made to develop young swimmers. The number of special swimming schools is constantly increasing. More swimming pools —indoor and outdoor ones—are being built in schools and recreation centers. The search for promising swimmers goes on everywhere, even in the far north, where all swimming has to be done indoors because of the climate.

Many of the sports schools are accommodated in separate buildings, others share facilities with Sports Societies for adult athletes. This is particularly the case with sports schools sponsored by such societies.

In rural areas, where the regular schools have more space, a sports school may use a school's grounds for playing fields and put up its own building for indoor training. Often the students themselves construct the building, lay out additional fields and courts, and install the equipment. In some rural areas, the state and collective farms are prosperous enough to support or help support their own sports schools. There are seven such schools in the Ukraine, the most productive agricultural area in the country.

A sports school may also be accommodated in a large Pioneer Palace—a recreational center that serves children of school age. Some boarding schools run a separate section as a sports school. And sports schools are also started in

A student at the tennis school, Miner, supported by a mine workers sports society.

Young athletes at a summer sports camp.

communities built around a large industrial enterprise. In such cases, it is the Trade Union Council that sponsors the school. Here, too, the school might be built by the students themselves, very likely with the help of their worker parents. Coaches are hired, and some are recruited from among the experienced sportsmen (holding a Master of Sports rating), on the work force. In such schools the sports taught are those in which the local children have the greatest interest.

Most of the sports schools eventually acquire their own summer training camps. Others rent the facilities of regular children's camps for training purposes. Country schools may also be rented for the summer. The students spend from three to seven weeks at these camps in intensive sports training and in the other typical camp activities. The work of the camp is done by the students and their coaches. A regulated program of training is followed, but the campers have plenty of time for fun, games, and side trips.

This year-round training of the schools and camps prepares the young athletes to compete with groups from other sports schools. Sometimes teams travel to unfamiliar cities and other national Soviet republics. There, in addition to the sports competition, they are taken to the local historical landmarks and museums. In this way, a young athlete may do a good deal of interesting traveling, widen his knowledge of his country, and enjoy many of the different customs and cultures within the Soviet Union.

To make sure that the sports school students keep up their grades at their regular schools, do well in their athletic training, and get leaves of absence for out-of-town contests, they are trained to budget their time and energies with utmost care. The young people have frequent group discussions with their coaches, exchanging ideas about how to economize on both. When necessary, a student's coach may have private talks with him about this matter.

The extremely hard work and self-discipline that the sports school training calls for stands the students in good stead in competitions. They learn early to act like champions: "To give it all they've got, until there's nothing held back. Everything they've ever worked for, ever struggled for, is there, in the race, in the game. Everything."

With so many expensively equipped and staffed sports schools offering free training to such large numbers of young people, who pays the bills? The majority of the schools are financed by city, regional, republic, and central government agencies from their public health and educa-

Student athletes in their physics class at a sports boarding school.

tional budgets. Over a third of the schools are financed by the sports societies of trade and professional unions and other large-scale organizations. Such facilities for the sports schools as large pools and stadiums are built with money from sports lotteries, which are called in Russian *Sportloto,* meaning "Sports Bingo."

A closer look at several DIUSH's, each specializing in a different sport, reveals how the schools work on an everyday practical level.

3

A School for Greco-Roman Wrestlers

THIS "SCHOOL WITHOUT DESKS" HAS RECENTLY MOVED INTO its new quarters, a remodeled building in a new community on the outskirts of Moscow. The sign on the street side of the freshly painted structure reads: CHILDREN'S AND TEENAGERS' SCHOOL FOR CLASSICAL WRESTLING. Under the name, in smaller print, is an inscription indicating that this school's sponsoring organization is The City Council of *Burevestnik* and its sports society, *Nauka.**

The entrance is to the side, from a large sports compound, fenced off from the street. In this parklike area stand several other buildings that accommodate schools for free wrestling, boxing, figure skating, speed skating, basketball, and volleyball.

---

* The word *Nauka* means "knowledge." The building belongs to *Burevestnik*, the Educational Workers and University Students Union, which also finances the school.

35

Although it was a dismal, late-fall afternoon, windy and sleety, the day I visited, the boys kept pouring into their wrestling school. Inside it was warm and orderly. A relaxed atmosphere of busyness, concentration, and even a little mischief prevailed.

Most of the boys looked like typical working-class youngsters, for the neighborhood is largely inhabited by families of skilled and unskilled laborers.

Four hundred students, aged eleven to eighteen, are enrolled here. For six months to a year and a half after a student enters the school, depending on his physical development, he spends most of his time doing special exercises and playing certain games that will toughen him and increase his speed and ability to react quickly. Before he starts his wrestling training, he has to be in good physical shape.

The full course of training lasts up to seven years. The lessons are standardized and given in an official syllabus. These lessons begin with the most elementary rules of the Greco-Roman style of wrestling and move on to the finest points of technique that an expert wrestler must know.

A training session at the Nauka *School for Classical Wrestling in Moscow.*

The training and use of equipment are free. The boys pay only a slight membership fee to the sponsoring Sports Society—30 kopecks (35 cents) a year.

Twenty-five of the country's leading Greco-Roman wrestlers began their training in this school.

Mark Portugal, the director and head coach, is sure he now has among his students a future Olympic champion. A short and stocky man of about forty, Portugal has been a wrestling coach for nearly half of his life. He is a former wrestler, has a degree in Physical Education with a major in wrestling, is a Master of Sports, and has earned the title of Honored Coach, which means he is an outstanding coach.

The boy whom Portugal is sure will be a champion is named Sergei. Portugal first noticed him four years ago in a basketball game. The coach noticed the boy's heavy build and speed. He spoke to the boy about classical wrestling— the skill, the challenge, the satisfactions of the sport. Sergei was then a very shy boy without much self-confidence. It took a lot of persuading to get him to enroll in the school. But at last he agreed to give it a try. He soon began to enjoy wrestling and to become skillful at it.

Then there was some difficulty in his family—both of his parents became invalids. Sergei was needed at home. He stayed away from the school for a year. When he showed up again, unexpectedly, he had gained twenty kilograms and had grown a foot. To Portugal he looked more than ever like a future champion. The boy took up training again with new enthusiasm. And by the time I saw him he was seventeen and seemed ready to take on anyone in the world.

Sergei, 17, the star student at the Nauka *School for Classical Wrestling in Moscow.*

Just the same, Sergei does not plan to devote the rest of his life to wrestling. After finishing the basic Soviet eight-year school, he enrolled in a technical school to study motion picture photography. He has made up his mind to become a cameraman. He likes art and says that he hopes to use film photography to "test his artistic abilities." But he also loves wrestling and works very hard at it.

Mark Portugal was clearly proud of his school and his boys. He and the other coaches were obviously dedicated to the aims of their work. They emphasized that they took an interest in each student, regardless of his capabilities in wrestling. They felt they were there also to help the boys grow up, to mature into competent young people. They were also there to help "troubled" boys, the ones with behavior problems in the regular school or at home, or both. They befriend such boys and try to help them while they train them in wrestling. As one of the coaches put it: "In a way we teach them to wrestle with their problems as well as with another wrestler. After a while they gain self-confidence and learn how to get along with others." The coaches make it their business to find out about a "difficult" boy's family circumstances. There are sometimes situations in which it is a parent that is causing the trouble, and the coaches try to change such a parent's attitude toward the son.

The coaches also spoke about runts—undersized, scrawny boys who come to the school to learn wrestling. It gives them great satisfaction to see such boys grow strong in body

The director of the Nauka *School for Classical Wrestling having fun with his students at their summer training camp in Estonia.*

and in a sense of self-worth under their guidance. Mr. Portugal put it this way: "Our task is not necessarily to make great wrestlers out of our boys. It is as much to change the weak and discouraged ones into healthy, strong, and hopeful young men."

The boys attend the school from six to twelve hours a week, depending on the age group they are in. The oldest have the longest and the most frequent sessions. Every boy who has started his training in wrestling must take part in competitions. At the age of fourteen, they begin to travel to other cities and republics for matches. The students have to pass examinations in wrestling techniques. They receive grades. Those who fail and cannot do better, are dropped and advised to take up another sport for which they are physically better suited. This happens to few.

The school has a huge gymnasium, newly equipped. A dark green mat covers the entire floor. It is spotlessly clean. The boys work out with mustard-colored dummies of various weights and sizes, or they wrestle with each other. Except for a couple of eleven-year-olds (*novichki*—newcomers), whose wrestling looked more like puppy play, the boys seemed to be taking their workouts seriously. There was no horseplay, aimless running, fighting, or shouting. Hardly any sounds could be heard besides the hard breathing and panting of the young wrestlers. The coaches moved among the pairs, making comments in low voices. There seemed to be no occasion for scolding or threatening, or even blowing a whistle for order.

The 400 boys had come to the school because they liked wrestling. But many planned careers in fields other than sports. Even the two *novichki* had future plans. I asked eleven-year-old Rashid, a little Tatar, who his favorite hero was. Raising his dark eyes to the ceiling and thinking hard, he soon answered that it was the writer, Gorky. What did Rashid hope to be when he grew up? "A writer," he answered softly. His wrestling mate, Kol 'ka, said that Yuri Gagarin (the first man in space) was his hero. Would he like to be a cosmonaut when he grew up? Kol 'ka's answer was yes, if they would take him; if they didn't, he might be happy to become a "very great wrestler."

In the summer many of the boys go to a training camp with their coaches. The ones who have done very well and

Seriozha and his guitar—at the summer training camp for students of the Nauka *School for Classical Wrestling.*

those who need a great deal more concentrated training are the first to be selected. They spend 52 days at the camp, dividing the time between regular wrestling periods and the usual camp activities for fun and relaxation. One summer the school hired a camp in the Baltic Soviet republic, Estonia. This gave the boys a chance to visit a Soviet area quite unlike their own Moscow region. They enjoyed the Baltic seashore and had a chance to hear some of Estonia's famous choral singing, when they attended the yearly Song Festival in which 30,000 children participated.

The parents pay one-third of the cost of the boy's being at camp if they can afford it. Otherwise it is free. As is the custom, all the work at camp is done by the boys and their coaches.

The boys plan to do most of the work in keeping up and improving their new school in the city, too. They are going to set up a snack bar, decorate and furnish a visitors' room, with a silver *samovar* (the typical Russian tea urn) for treating guests to tea, and they will put up a glass-brick wall over which they will arrange ivy plants. The surrounding walls they hope to fill with cases full of trophies, photographs of famous graduates from their school, and other symbols of its achievements in Greco-Roman wrestling.

4

A School for Acrobatic Gymnastics

SINCE 1952, THE YEAR IN WHICH THE UNION OF SOVIET SO-cialist Republics participated in the Olympic Games for the first time, Soviet girl gymnasts have been winning medals and delighting viewers. Teenagers like Olga Korbut and Ludmilla Turischeva, who were the two most out-standing gymnasts at the 1972 Summer Olympics, have amazed the sports world, performing with the grace of dancers and the skill of circus acrobats. Boy and girl gym-nasts are trained in Sports Schools for Acrobatic Gymnastics. The period of training is at least five years. Their remark-able ability is due not only to their natural athletic talents and their expert coaches, but also to the *scientific* system of training they get at these special schools.

The planning of the programs of these schools is done by the USSR Gymnastics Federation. Its syllabus details just how children are to be introduced to the exercises and the

Ludmilla Turischeva, all-around World Champion Gymnast, performing on the 4-inch beam at the 1972 summer Olympics, where she won a gold medal.

Olga Korbut, teenage Olympic champion, gold medalist in acrobatic gymnastics, 1972.

stunts on the bars, balance beam, rings, horse and other equipment that are a part of the sport of gymnastics. The proof of the skill with which this systematic method of training has been devised is in the achievements of such very young gymnasts as Nina Dronova. At the age of fourteen, Nina ranked among the world's top gymnasts. She had already earned numerous awards in the Soviet Union and in Japan. In the junior competitions of the USSR People's Games, in the summer of 1971, when she was thirteen, Nina won first place in every event and was one of the few gymnasts to receive 10 points, the highest possible score, for her performance in free exercises. At the international contest in Nagoya, Japan, held in 1971, she took first place after scoring 38.15 points in the multiple event —.05 of a point higher than the score of Soviet world title holder, Ludmilla Turischeva.

Tamara Lazakovich is another teenager who has won world championships in acrobatic gymnastics. She hails

Tamara Lazakovich, European champion gymnast surrounded by admiring fans, themselves trainees in gymnastics.

from Belorussia, a Soviet Republic in the western part of European Russia. Tamara became interested in acrobatics at the age of eight. At fourteen she was the youngest Master of Sports in gymnastics, and soon after won the junior championship of the Soviet Union. She is noted for her good proportions, purity of lines, athletic control, and remarkable plasticity. In 1970, at the age of fifteen, she won the national championship on the beam, the trickiest piece of apparatus. The next year she won a world championship with a gold medal for her team victory, and became the all-around champion gymnast of the USSR. Tamara has had the same coach since 1964.

"Outwardly," her coach said, "Tamara appears rather calm and withdrawn, but inside her everything seems to boil." A normal day's work for her, he discloses, would be polishing up 810 exercises and performing 22 full combinations. (A combination is a group of demanding exercises, often original with the athlete.)

To win their championships, gymnasts have to show originality as well as uncommon skill. They have to compose original routines and combinations for their performances, and choose those which show their athleticism and grace to best advantage. For instance, Olga Korbut's astounding flip on the 4-inch wide balance beam and her somersault in the air from the high crossbar helped her win her Olympic gold medal in 1972. She was the very first gymnast even to do that kind of flip.

The quest for originality, no matter the cost in hard work and risk, has led young Soviet male gymnasts to perform such original feats at world sports events that they have contributed to international gymnastics terminology.

At the 1952 Olympics, in Helsinki, non-Russian sports-men and trainees noticed certain routines performed by Soviet gymnasts that they had not seen before. Among these were "Russian circles" on the horse and "Russian turns" on the horizontal bars. At the 1954 World Championship, in Rome, the gymnast, Grant Shaginyan, won the gold medal for an extraordinary performance on the horse—he ended his routine with 360-degree turns. Ever since then, this Shaginyan stunt has been used in various combinations on this apparatus by all champions.

Albert Azaryan amazed gymnasts with a cross on the rings, which he was the first to do with an especially difficult combination.

A girl trainee being coached at a sports school in Armenia. Its director is former Olympic champion gymnast, Grant Shaginyan.

Twice Olympic champion, gymnast Albert Azarian, coaching his son, Eduard, at the sports school of which he is the director.

Former world champion, acrobat Mikhail Voronin, coaching a student at a sports school for gymnasts.

Mikhail Voronin introduced the "Voronin flip"—a flip on the rings ending in a straight-arm hand stand.

Sergei Diomidov was the first to execute a turn on the parallel bars ending in a one-hand stand—a feat still called the "Diomidov element."

Victor Klimenko, at the age of eighteen, became the Soviet champion in the long-horse vault. His routines are said to be the most complicated in the world, including cascades of high jumps.

Most of the Soviet champion gymnasts began their serious training as children at a Sports School for Acrobatics. These schools enroll both boys and girls. A number of spacious gymnasiums serve the several hundred children and teen-agers training in a Leningrad school for gymnasts. The gymnasium I visited was so large that it looked almost empty although 48 children were exercising in it that after-noon. There were five coaches working with individual students or with small groups.

The director of the school proudly told of the accom-plishments of the coaches. Among them was a former world champion, a pair of Honored Coaches, and a number of Physical Culture Institute graduates with Master's degrees.

The school's several hundred boys and girls trained in the usual three age groups: ten to eleven, twelve to thir-teen, fourteen to fifteen. They attended training sessions two or three times a week for a total of four to nine hours.

Members of the youngest group have to master the stand-ard acrobatic movements, and when they do, they earn the lowest sports rating (No. 3). The children in the second age group have to learn more difficult routines and compose their own combinations. They also have to do exercises that involve groups and couples. This group starts to ap-pear in demonstrations and competitions. At the end of the second year of training in this age group, the students have to pass the tests for the second sports rating (No. 2). The oldest group masters the more difficult combinations and learns how to assist coaches of younger children in gymnas-tics clubs. At the end of their training, they have to pass the highest teenage rating (No. 1); the more capable ones may try for the rating of Master of Sports.

The groups are limited to fifteen to twenty students.

An aspiring gymnast taking his first lesson at a sports school in Soviet Georgia.

Boy gymnasts at a sports school in Armenia.

A student gymnast in a sports school in the city of Kuibyshev, on the Volga.

They train in smaller groups for the more difficult exercises and individually for complicated routines.

The students are assigned homework—exercises to be done outside of sports school. They are tested and graded on all of their work.

There are frequent medical checkups. The coaches keep in close touch with the examining physicians and know exactly the physical potential of each trainee.

Each two-hour session is divided into three parts: 15 to 20 minutes are devoted to warming-up and toughening exercises; 70 to 100 minutes to basic acrobatic exercises; 5 to 10 minutes for special stunts. During the longest part the children do free jumping, group, and class exercises. They use the various pieces of apparatus, perform field and track type of exercises, and play active sports games. The last and shortest part is devoted to posture exercises, dance steps for the girls, or exercises to relax the muscles. In the group exercises the athletes develop all kinds of acrobatic combinations, including the pyramid.

Some of the boys and girls in the Leningrad Gymnastics DIUSH were already gravity-defying young athletes. As the school's director looked on proudly, he no doubt already visualized some of them with champion's medals on their chests.

Student gymnasts exercising in the open at a sports camp.

5

A School for Artistic Gymnastics

EVERY AFTERNOON A STEADY STREAM OF GIRLS CARRYING dance-practice shoes enters one of the several buildings on Moscow's Lenin Hills. It is part of the recreation center for young people whose structures and athletic fields cover an area of twenty acres. The building to the left of the main one accommodates several sports schools. One of them is the special Sport School for Artistic Gymnastics. The girls with the dance-practice shoes are on their way to classes in this sport.

About 500 girls, seven to seventeen years of age, are enrolled in this school. Artistic gymnastics is quite different from the acrobatic variety. Only girls engage in this sport. They do not use bars, balance beams, rings, or any other stationary apparatus. Instead they use streamers, scarves, hoops, balls, and jump ropes in their practice and improvisations.

Lenochka and Marina, no-vichki—new students—at a school for artistic gymnastics in Moscow.

Exercises with streamers of ribbon at a school for artistic gymnastics in Moscow.

Olympiada Ershova, director of the leading Moscow school for artistic gymnastics, with her students.

Olympiada Ershova is the school's director and head coach. Hers is the leading school of its kind in the country. It serves as a model for other such schools in methods of training, standards, experiments, and innovations. From the description of her work and the goals of artistic gymnastics in general, it becomes clear that the object is not only to develop the girls' physical strength and gymnastic skills, but to give them grace and charm as well.

Mrs. Ershova invited me to visit her classes. The first one I observed had twenty-five girls in it, eight to nine years of age. They had just come from their twice-yearly medical checkup. The class was held in a very large gymnasium with parquet floors, and ceiling-high mirrors covering three of the walls. The bars stretching across the walls were the kind ballet students use for doing exercises. The mirrors were there so the young gymnasts could see how they looked as they practiced their exercises. The girls were dressed in bright blue leotards, black dance-practice shoes, and many had large bows in their braids or ponytails. They looked as poised as dancers.

An essential part of the kind of gymnastics they were learning is calisthenics. The word calisthenics comes from the Greek words for beauty and strength and the aim of the exercise is to develop bodily strength and beauty of movement. Mrs. Ershova explained that artistic gymnastics is considered a sport because it makes great demands on the gymnast's endurance, patience, stamina, and will to excel.

The overall goal is to train girls to move with great agility but always with grace and expressiveness; to teach them to plan calisthenic movements to music—movements that are lovely in their lightness, freedom, balance, intricacy, and elegance. Such training develops not only gymnastic coordination and control but also poise and charm.

"Feminine grace and charm add to the girl's social poise. The physical stamina she acquires prepares her for work and for easier child bearing," explained Mrs. Ershova.

Music is especially important in artistic gymnastics. Most of the exercises and routines are done to the accompaniment of classical music. The girls are trained to listen carefully to the music's rhythm and emotional expression, so as to better translate them into graceful exercises.

"When done well," said Olympiada Ershova, "artistic gymnastics is a joyous blending of dance and athletics." Several of her students have transferred to ballet schools. They were welcomed there and have done well.

The school employs three full-time pianists.

The several hundred girls in Mrs. Ershova's school had been carefully selected for their good health, slenderness, and good ear for music. However, applicants who do not meet the entrance requirements because of overweight or awkwardness are not turned away. They are formed into special groups with whom Mrs. Ershova works separately. "Many an ugly duckling," she said, smiling delightedly, "has changed into a lovely young swan before my eyes."

The regular students are divided into four age groups: seven to nine, ten to eleven, twelve to thirteen, and fourteen to sixteen. The youngest groups have no more than twenty to twenty-five girls; the oldest eight to ten. The youngest train twice a week for a total of 144 hours in the nine-month school year; the oldest groups, three times a

A second-year student at a school for artistic gymnastics in Moscow.

Grace and beauty—a gymnast practicing in the open at a sports school near Moscow.

A fourteen-year-old advance student at a school for artistic gymnastics in Moscow.

week for a total of 216 hours in the year.

As in the other sports schools, the girls begin to help teach others the elements of their sport soon after they start their own training. As a community service, they must help organize and train groups of girls in large apartment developments, in small recreation centers, and in gymnastic circles at the regular schools.

The older girls are called upon to tutor individually any young trainees who need additional help in mastering the more difficult exercises and combinations.

The program calls for a specific series of exercises and gymnastic feats for each of the groups. The girls gain in skill and control through participation in regularly scheduled competitions.

After the full course of training, lasting seven to eight years, the girls perform with the skill and self-assurance of

Girl gymnasts at a sports boarding school.

A beginner exercising in front of the mirror in the gymnasium of a school for artistic gymnastics.

good dancers and circus gymnasts. The popularity of the circus with the Russian people may inspire many children to become skilled gymnasts. Love of the dance is also practically universal in their country. Artistic gymnastics satisfies both of these national enthusiasms.

It is therefore not surprising that there are several hundred sports schools and thousands upon thousands of circles for this type of athletics. Girls are lured by the posters hung in their schools and club centers saying: "You too may become as fleet as a doe, as straight and tall as a poplar. Take up artistic gymnastics."

Training in this sport in the special sports schools and recreation clubs has been so beneficial that there are plans to introduce it in all the regular schools as part of the physical education program.

6

A Swimming School

WATER SPORTS ARE RELATIVELY NEW IN THE SOVIET UNION, at least in many parts of it. Until recently the country was not prosperous enough to build the expensive facilities needed for swimming, water polo, rowing, diving, canoeing, and other aquatic sports. In a country as cold as much of the USSR is, indoor facilities are needed if any kind of regular program is going to be started. The first national swimming competitions in the country were held in 1921. At that time there was not a single indoor swimming pool in the entire nation. The contestants had learned to swim in chilly Russian seas, rivers, and lakes.

Before the Second World War, not a single Russian had made a world swimming record. Soviet swimmers made their Olympic debut in 1952, in Helsinki, but their best performer, Maria Gavrish, ranked only sixth in the breast-stroke event. In the later 1950s, when the country had

Swimming students at a sports school in Kaluga.

somewhat recovered from the war and had rebuilt its ruined cities and industries, large-scale construction of indoor and outdoor swimming pools for year-round use was begun.

At the very next Olympic Games, held in Melbourne, Australia, in 1956, a Soviet male swimmer won a bronze medal for his performance in the 200-meter breaststroke. At the Tokyo Olympics, in 1964, Galina Prozumenshchikova and Georgi Prokopenko took first and second places in the 200-meter breaststroke. Galina was not yet sixteen when she won her gold medal.

Since then, Soviet swimmers have given a good account of themselves in both national and international events. By 1972 there were 1,450 first-class swimming pools in the Soviet Union. And the special Sports Schools for swimming and other aquatic sports had made good use of them.

The program of training at the swimming schools is intense. The junior swimming school, or Swimming DIUSH, on the Lenin Hills in Moscow serves children from seven to seventeen years of age. It is set up for a six-year training course. The best swimmers are selected for an additional training period of three years.

The school's pool is 80 x 45 feet and has six lanes. It is used from 7 A.M. to 10 P.M., seven days a week. Close to 1,200 children and teenagers swim in it daily.

From seven in the morning to two in the afternoon it is reserved for children from a number of regular schools. The schools bus their second graders to the pool for two weekly swimming lessons given by special coaches. (In the near future not only second, but also third, and fourth graders will receive 2 swimming lessons a week in this Swimming School). The course for the second graders lasts two months, then other children start coming for a similar 2-month course. The most promising swimmers are selected for training at the Swimming School.

In the school the youngsters make rapid progress. They swim a minimum of four hours a day, three times a week. In 1972 the school had 18 students who had earned Master of Sports ratings in swimming, and several had made the top national team.

The most promising swimmers go to a regular school near the Lenin Hills, so that they can come for their long swimming sessions without losing time in traveling. They swim from 8 A.M. to 10 A.M. and from 6 P.M. to 8 P.M. This regular school schedules classes so as to make it possible for the

Young swimmers and their coach in a house of sports in the remote Chuvash Autonomous Area, in the Middle Volga Region.

swimmers to take their training sessions without missing other classes. The regular school in Lenin Hills will eventually become a boarding school for the swimming trainees as well as for talented students in the soccer, volleyball, gymnastics, and bicycling sports schools in the complex.

The children who do not develop sufficient speed and strength for competition, or who lose interest in the sport, may be dropped by recommendation of the Coaches Council. But they may be encouraged to learn water polo, skin diving, or canoeing and then may be transferred to groups for these aquatic sports.

An indoor pool for practice in rowing at a Ukranian college of physical culture.

Some of the swimmers go to summer training camp. Out of the 30,000 Moscow young people in swimming schools, 150 are selected to go to camp. Here, they swim at least four hours a day. They are fed an especially nourishing diet, nap two hours a day, and wrestle and play energetic ball games to increase their stamina. They enjoy four free hours daily. Bedtime is at 10 P.M.

The same rigorous program of year-round training is followed in all the major swimming schools.

Out of the 500 best students, two or three are chosen to compete in European or International events.

Concentrated training such as is given at the special schools for swimmers creates problems for young athletes who are also interested in other fields. Dmitri, for example, has worked hard with the same coach for six years and has done very well. The coach is convinced he can make him into an Olympic swimmer. But Dmitri is also gifted in mathematics and attends a special school for students who excel in this subject. His father is a Professor of Physics at Moscow University. He wants his son to drop swimming so he can spend more time on his majors in mathematics and science. Dmitri is of two minds, but he told his coach that he will not go against his father's will. The coach is, of course, very disappointed.

On the other hand, the attitude of Nina Petrovna, an Olympic swimmer at the age of fifteen, is typical of those sports school trainees who choose to devote all the time necessary to their sport to succeed. In an interview she gave before leaving Moscow to participate in the 1972 Summer Olympics, she said:

Fifteen of the 1200 workers' children who attend the sports school sponsored by the plant's sports society.

I'm in the ninth grade. I have to work terribly hard to get decent grades and to make progress in my swimming at the same time. But it's worth it—I love sports! I started with skiing, but soon decided that I love swimming best. I enjoy the training although it is often terribly exhausting. I have always liked the breaststroke best of all. I earned the Master of Sports rank in this form when I was twelve. But I hated the backstroke—water always got up my nose and I'd lose my breath. I struggled and struggled with this problem for many months. There were days when I'd be very discouraged. But what a joy it was to feel suddenly that I had finally got the thing right. I was blissfully sure that I had when I won, and even established a new Soviet record, in a European competition in a multiple-form event. I was fourteen then and received the International Master of Sports rating. Now I'm about to leave for the Olympics. I'm very worried—American and Australian girls are marvelous swimmers and the strongest opponents. I find the challenge thrilling, though.

The heavy program of training does not eliminate all fun at the swimming schools. At the Moscow school the younger students celebrate the New Year holiday by anchoring a New Year's tree in the swimming pool. They have a party in the water, play water games, masquerade as sea creatures. The older students travel to meets and delight in the change of scenery and the excitement of competitions. And like healthy young boys and girls the world over, they enjoy applying their abundant energies to excelling in their favorite sport.

7

The Chess Schools

CHESS IS THE THIRD MOST POPULAR NATIONAL PASTIME IN the Soviet Union—soccer and hockey being the first two. In Russia, chess is considered a sport even though it exercises mental muscles rather than the physical ones. It is held to be a sport because it calls for intensive training and concentration, great skill, and strong determination to win. As in other sports, Soviet chess players are *amateurs* because they earn their living at other occupations.

Russian players have not always participated in world title matches. The first world-title competition took place in 1851, and in 1866 an official world champion was acknowledged for the first time. He was Wilhelm Steinitz of Prague, Czechoslovakia. Steinitz held the crown for twenty-eight years. It was during this period that modern tournament chess developed, and among the challengers of Steinitz was a Russian, Mikhail Tchigorin, who originated many of the plays that his countrymen have since followed.

A German, Dr. Emanuel Lasker, defeated Steinitz, in 1894; and he was in turn defeated by a Cuban, José Raoul Capablanca, in 1921. A Russian, Alexander Alekhine, won the world crown in 1927 and held it until 1935. (Alekhine was a Russian but not a Soviet citizen, having emigrated after the Revolution, but his game had some of the elements preferred by Russian players.)

Meanwhile, within the Soviet Union, chess was becoming a very popular sport. A fourteen-year-old Leningrad school-boy, Mikhail Botvinnik, won a dramatic game from Champion Capablanca in 1925. At twenty-one, Botvinnik beat Alekhine. He won the World Championship in 1948 (and held it until 1957). From that time on, for twenty-four consecutive years, Soviet players held the world crown— until Bobby Fischer won it in Reykjavik, Iceland, from Boris Spassky, in 1972.

The world championship among women chess players is held by a Soviet woman from the Republic of Georgia, Nona Gaprindashvili.

Experts agree that there are special reasons for Soviet supremacy in chess. They say that no society has ever invested such energies in the perfection of a pastime. It can also be said that in no country has chess become such a mass sport involving so many children. Since millions of children play chess, it is possible to select a large number of very gifted ones and give them special training. The making of chess champions starts in the special Chess Schools.

The Chess Schools are organized in the same way as the special schools for other sports. They are subsidized by the government and the mass sports societies.

An applicant must pass an aptitude test and must attend a set number of sessions per week, regularly. He must take part in competitions and show a steady improvement in his playing. He is expected to devote himself to learning the plays of notable chess players. The young students are tested and receive ratings and classifications in accordance with their performance.

The usual ratio of boys to girls is 4 to 1.

The two outstanding training centers are the Leningrad Chess School for Children and Youth, and the Moscow Chess School on the Lenin Hills. These train the most gifted young people and experiment in training methods, passing on to the other chess schools the results of their experiences.

World Champions Mikhail Botvinnik and Boris Spassky began their training in the Leningrad school. In a number of ways, Spassky's story is representative of the road traveled by all Soviet chess stars. Born in Leningrad in 1937, he started playing chess at the age of five, although his city was under siege and he had been evacuated and was living in circumstances of constant danger and a lack of adequate food. Soon after the end of the war, in 1946, when he was nine years old, he was brought back to Leningrad. He then began training in the Leningrad Chess School. He showed such unusual ability that a very skilled teacher was immediately assigned to him. At the age of ten, he won a "best game" prize in the Junior Championship of the Russian Chess Federation, and at twelve he was Junior Champion of Leningrad.

*Sergei Soloviev, a fifth-grade chess player from Moscow, compet-
ing in the 11th National College Students Tournament.*

*Young students at the chess school in Leningrad, where Mikhail
Botvinnik and Boris Spassky, both former world champions,
trained.*

Anatoli Karpov, the new Soviet chess genius and grandmaster, being groomed to play Bobby Fischer.

Now some of the big names in Soviet chess, including Botvinnik, began to help him. In school he excelled in athletics, and at college he took a major in journalism. But chess was his main interest, and he has said: "I regularly played up to five hours a day." At the age of sixteen he was awarded the title of Chess Master by the International Chess Federation, and at eighteen he became the youngest Grandmaster in the history of the game, after meeting all opposition and winning the title of Junior World Champion. They were already calling him "the next Capablanca."

Soon after Spassky lost his world crown to Fischer, a new star emerged—Anatoli Karpov. Karpov, too, was trained at the Leningrad school. At twenty-one, Karpov shared first place in the Alekhine Memorial Tournament in November 1972; he shared first place in the Hastings Tournament in England with Viktor Korchnoi, another Soviet player, less than a month later; and a few months earlier, in July, he scored 7 points out of 9, leading the Soviet Student Team to victory in the World Students Championship; finally, he made a 9–2 score in the finals of the 1972 Olympiad.

Anatoli's work at the Leningrad chess school enabled him, at the age of thirteen, to embark on a mature study of the games of the former Cuban champion, Capablanca, admired by Soviet players for the simplicity and clarity of his moves. Though Anatoli is said to be shy and unassuming, he does not seem to lack self-confidence. When asked if he thought himself capable of becoming the next chess king, Anatoli replied, softly, "Evidently, I shall."

The Leningrad Chess School may have produced a Botvinnik, a Spassky, and a Karpov, but the leading Chess School of Moscow, on the Lenin Hills, also trains its students to reach great heights. It has contributed its share of young Masters of Chess and a sprinkling of Grandmasters.

Usually this school registers 200 students each September. A month after Spassky lost his crown, 500 boys and girls, seven to seventeen years of age, clamored to be admitted into the school—the largest number ever to apply. Two-hundred and fifty passed the stringent examination and were accepted. The rest were distributed among the chess groups in the Sports Clubs run by the Pioneer organization, with the promise that when they reached a certain level of performance they could reapply to the chess school.

When I paid a visit to the Moscow school, no sooner had I shaken hands with the director, than he showed me a book. It was a translation into Russian of Bobby Fischer's *My Sixty Memorable Plays*. Fifty thousand copies of the Russian edition were published immediately after the World Championship Games in the summer of 1972. They were sold out in one day!

Every one of the forty tables in the main game room at the school was occupied by boys and girls deeply engrossed in their games. The director said that all of them were studying Fischer's book.

The 350 students at this school include 30 girls. All students are divided into 21 groups, according to experience and age. The younger groups are instructed two to three periods a week, each lasting 45 minutes. The oldest students put in as much as twelve periods a week.

The coaches of the younger groups are generally schoolteachers who love chess and have won high ratings in the game; most have also taken special training courses in chess at a Sports Institute. The older boys and girls are coached by outstanding players, some of them Grandmasters.

The entire school participates in the annual national matches held in May.

The school trains coaches for small chess schools and for chess clubs in the various recreational centers for young people.

So much for the two major chess schools. Now we shall see how an average school is run. The Georgian Chess School, located in a community built around a railroad junction far from the republic's capital, has 120 students

Former world champion, Tigran Petrosian, analyzes a game played by students of the chess school on the Lenin Hills in Moscow.

seven to fifteen years of age. It has existed for 25 years. Among its graduates is Nona Gaprindashvili, the World Champion (1972) among women chess players. In summarizing his school's program, the director, Mikhail Shishov, said:

Our 120 chess lovers become acquainted with the theory of the game, solve difficult problems, analyze the plays of famous Chess Masters. Their theoretical knowledge is tested in the games, the ones they play with one another and in the many matches and tournaments played elsewhere. We must accomplish one more important task—our children must fulfill their social obligations by helping train chess enthusiasts in the various chess clubs at schools and in the Pioneer Houses. They help organize the "White Castle" tournaments, whose participants often number in the thousands.

The heroes of Soviet chess actively participate in training and inspiring young players to reach superior levels of skill. At the competition held in 1972 among the chess schools run by six Palaces of Pioneers—the ones in Leningrad, Moscow, Tbilisi (Georgia), Kiev (Ukraine), Riga (Latvia), and Chelyabinsk (Western Siberia)—all the captains of the teams were Grandmasters who had begun their serious training in chess in these cities. Three of them were former World Champions and one was the then current World Champion.

Chess is popularized through books on the history of the

The matches for the school's championship are in full swing at an Estonian chess school.

game, on tactics, and through biographies of famous players. It is not uncommon for 200,000 copies of a book to be issued in a first edition. One such publication, *Fun with Chess,* by M. Yudovich, is a collection of famous games, amusing adventures in chess, astounding moves. It also offers quotations of the opinions of famous men who have loved the game. Pablo Neruda, a Chilean who won a Nobel Prize for Poetry, is quoted as saying, "What is chess? It is one of the human victories over oneself—for me chess is poetry—the poetry of struggle between the mind and the will to win." The Russian composer Sergei Prokofiev, says, "Chess transports me into a unique world—the world where plans are locked in battle with the passion to win." *Fun with Chess* also offers such items as the fact that the number of moves that can be made with the thirty-two pieces on the sixty-four squares of the board is $7,534,686,312,361,225,307 \times 10^{33}$.

Chess is widely popularized over children's radio and television programs. A television chess school, conducted under the guidance of several regular chess schools, has 3,000 registered students. It holds classes twice a week. The instruction is given by a Grandmaster, assisted by one of his young students, already a Master of Chess. Assignments are given, the answers sent in to the television station, and tests are administered. This school tries to reach young enthusiasts who live in areas where chess schools or clubs are not easy to set up.

The monthly magazine *Pioner* (Pioneer), with a circulation of 7.5 million among children ten to fifteen years of age, conducts an informal chess school. It devotes the last one or two pages of every monthly issue to chess. In charge of the magazine's "school" in the paper is an imaginary puppetlike character named Peshkin.* Peshkin knows everything there is to know about chess. He travels to tournaments, reports on winning teams, challenges his readers to solve tricky problems, and gives out assignments, even during vacation months.

* "Peshkin" is derived from the word *peshka,* meaning "pawn."

The position of the pieces in a game played in his childhood by a world champion. (He played the white.) Similar games analyzed at chess schools.

Two girl chess enthusiasts with Peshkin.

Peshkin's pages were especially exciting in the November 1970, issue of the magazine. He was shown on a schooner, speeding to the second national "White Castle" tournament, in which close to half a million young chess lovers participated. His report was published in that November issue. He listed the winning teams and congratulated the youngest groups for their good showing. The winning teams were identified by town, school, and the names of the players and coaches. There was a photo of Alesha Ilyn, a ten-year-old boy from Leningrad, who was the youngest player to reach the finals. Peshkin disclosed that Alesha had not one but two teachers—his father and his grandmother. When his father, who is a geologist, went on field trips, his grandmother took over the coaching. Alesha played so well at the tournament that Peshkin was glad to award him a super-prize—the "Certificate of the Bishop and the Castle." The names of the five boys who sent in the best solutions to the previous issue's problems were also mentioned. Thousands of chess enthusiasts and readers of the *Pioner* probably turn first to the back pages when the magazine arrives to see if *their* name has been mentioned by Peshkin.

Among the unusual methods used in the Chess Schools to train young people, is regular physical exercise. Coaches believe that exercising and strengthening the body helps relax and strengthen the mind.

Soviet boys seem to have no prejudice toward girl chess players. They even accept a woman as coach. A chess group of thirty-five boys and five girls at a Pioneer Palace in Tashkent, Uzbekistan (a Central Asian Soviet Republic), is coached by Alli Mkhtygli, a twenty-one-year-old Master of Chess. Alli's father trained her. He was himself an Honored Coach, and when he began to teach her, she turned out to be a very good pupil, earning her own Master of Chess rank at the age of eighteen.

Some foreign commentators on Soviet chess attribute its popularity to the long Russian winters, when it is too cold to do anything but sit near the fire and play chess. But one Soviet chess reporter suggested that if this were the most important reason for the popularity of chess, Greenland would lead every other nation. As a matter of fact, no season is without its chess activity in the USSR. Summer camps employ chess coaches, and there are usually lively matches at the end of the camp season. Nor are the young people tired of chess when registration begins in September at the chess schools. There is never a lack of applicants.

And to make sure that the number of enthusiasts will grow, there is a trend to teach chess to preschoolers. The chess pieces designed especially for them are large and solid, almost as large as the children themselves. As they push them around their huge boards, they seem to exercise their physical and mental muscles at the same time.

Every modern invention possible is put to use in the training of young chess students. In the Soviet Union, as well as in the United States, a chess computer has been invented. Ex-World Champion Botvinnik, now a cybernetics scientist, is working on improvements for it. The computer is expected to reveal the thought processes of chess players. A better knowledge of these processes would give the player a better idea of how his opponent is likely to move. This ultramodern device is named after the ancient Goddess of chess, *Caissa*.

But, however they are trained, Soviet children are talented and are often an embarrassment to veteran players. Mikhail Tahl, Grandmaster and former Soviet world champion, has said: "I have had numerous opponents in games of simultaneous play in many foreign countries. I discovered in those places that the most dangerous opponents belong to the generation that has just begun to shave. But the Grandmasters and Masters in my country experience their most humiliating defeats at the hands of knee-pants adversaries."

A chess lesson at a kindergarten.

8

The Sports School Training of a Soccer Star

WHAT THE RUSSIANS (AND MOST OTHER NATIONS) CALL "FOOT-ball" is what Americans call soccer. The Russian version of the game is played according to the international rules for soccer-football. In the Soviet Union the game is called "football," spelled with Russian letters, and the players are "footballers."

In the USSR, as in close to 100 nations, football is the most popular sport. The reason for this is that the game provides a high degree of open play, body contact, skill, swift action, individual cunning, teamwork, and thrills. (Ice hockey runs a close second in challenge and excitement.)

Football is a goal game. The object is to propel a round ball toward the opponents' goal and between his goalposts by kicking or dribbling the ball with the feet, the head, or any part of the body except the arms and hands. One player only—the goalkeeper—is allowed to use his hands on the ball—and then only when he is in his own penalty area. Each goal has two goalposts 8 feet high. The posts are placed 8 feet apart and are connected by a crossbar at the top. A goal net is attached to the rear. The playing field is 120 yards by 75 yards, maximum; 100 yards by 55 yards, minimum. The ball has a circumference of 27 to 28 inches and is made of inflated leather or rubber. The regulation leather shoes are high laced and cleated with leather or rubber to protect the player against slipping. The player wears shin guards under his knee-length socks.

Each of the two teams has eleven players: a goalkeeper; two fullbacks, right and left; three halfbacks, right, center,

A young Uzbek football goalie.

A grandmother soccer fan gives her grandson a last-minute pointer before the match.

and left; five forwards—outside right, inside right, center, inside left and outside left.

A goal scores 1 point. The game lasts 90 minutes with a 10-minute break between halves.

Sports Schools for Football are set up for boys as young as eleven. Training can continue to the age of eighteen.

Vladimir Pulghin is a famous Soviet footballer. He began to play his favorite game in his backyard before he was old enough for first grade. By the age of twelve he was playing adult football with a fine boys' team. It was summertime and the boys had been lucky enough to find a very good coach. They played on the field of a recreation center. But the summer came to an end, and the coach had to bid them goodbye until the following year.

Toward the end of September, Vladimir happened to read a notice that the special Soccer School in his area had started its registration. He lived in a mining and steel manufacturing center in the Dniepropetrovsk region.

Several hundred boys showed up for the entrance screening. Many more came than there was room for in the school. First there was a strict medical examination. This was followed by a physical aptitude test for agility, quickness, coordination of movement. Finally, the examining coach looked at the boys' regular school record, checking on their grades and conduct. Then he announced the names of those who were accepted. Vladimir was among them.

At first the several weekly sessions were a great disappointment to him. They consisted of seemingly endless running, jumping, gymnastics, and exercises calling for instant responses to tricky situations. The ball came into play only at the end of each day's work, if at all.

Time passed. The lessons gradually became more varied and more interesting. Vladimir's group was taught technique, tactics and an understanding of all the complicated rules of the game. The coach thought up more and more difficult play situations, challenging the boys to solve them. He was a good coach but hard. He didn't tolerate laziness, halfhearted endeavor, or lack of discipline. At the end of each week, each student had to give an account of himself, not only on the playing field but in theory as well.

Vladimir did well enough to be allowed to play on strong outside teams a year before he graduated. His graduation came four years after he started at the school. After that, he played on one major team after another—first for his city, then for his region, and later for his republic, the Ukraine. He developed into a powerful goalie and his coaches predicted that he would be selected for a national team.

Then it happened. Vladimir hurt his hand badly. The doctors told him to forget about football forever. They said he would never again be a goalkeeper. He ignored this, however, and kept in good physical condition by doing hours of exercises daily while his hand improved. It gradually healed. And soon he began to play again at the goal. Lev Yashin, one of the nation's greatest goalies, had heard of Vladimir's misfortune, and of his courage and determination. He admired not only the younger footballer's skill but his will to succeed. Yashin invited him to play on his own team, the unmatched Moscow "Dynamos."

The No. 1 goalkeeper took a personal interest in Vladimir's progress, helping him improve his game. On one occasion the younger player was given a chance to substitute for the remarkable Yashin. Playing too impulsively, Vladimir lost the game for the previously unbeatable Muscovites. But he didn't lose heart. In subsequent games he showed how well he had learned his lesson. He always thought before moving, no matter how instantaneous his reaction had to be. And Yashin remained confident that his protégé would succeed. He had proved that he was a player with character as well as talent—a player who didn't crack up in defeat but learned from it.

Not long afterward, Lev Yashin resigned his goalkeeper's post and "willed" it to his "heir," Vladimir Pulghin. The new star has helped the team maintain its great record.

Boys all over the Soviet Union know of Vladimir Pulghin and others like him. While they enjoy their games, they hope that they, too, may prove to be as determined and successful.

9

The Sports "Sections" for Children and Teenagers

THE SEVERAL THOUSAND SPORTS SCHOOLS (DIUSH'S) TRAIN THE cream of the crop of promising young athletes. They generally make their facilities available to children and teenagers whose interest in their chosen sport is keen and whose physical stamina and special aptitudes are considerably above average. And they can serve only those young people who are fortunate enough to live within walking or reasonable traveling distance from a school that specializes in their chosen sport. But there are many thousands of other young people wanting to be trained in their favorite sport whose physical fitness is not outstanding or who do not have access to a sports school.

For them there is another type of training available, in centers called *Sports Sections*.

Twenty-nine million schoolchildren eleven to fifteen years of age belong to the Pioneer Organization. This means

An aspiring goalie at a Sports Section in the city of Kuibyshev, on the Volga.

that this many children belong to Pioneer groups in their regular schools, are members of interest clubs in a neighborhood House of Pioneers, or join a Pioneer Palace for their out-of-school activities—a Pioneer Palace being a huge center for all kinds of recreational training, with excellent facilities and professional instructors.

Within the framework of these very numerous Pioneer groups in schools—both city and rural—and in the urban and rural Houses and Palaces of Pioneers, athletic training is offered on a vast scale. A number of groups, each for a different sport, make up a *Sports Section*.

Such Sections may be set up on the premises of regular schools or in the Pioneer recreational centers themselves. The various Sports Societies also establish Sports Sections for the young.

Students in Sports Sections are trained by professional coaches, who are sometimes assisted by older students from a Sports School (DIUSH).

The planned programs of training, the equipment, and the standards of achievement in the Sections aim to be on a level with those in the Sports Schools. Whether or not they are, depends on the locality, and the availability of adequate space and good coaches. The objective, however, is to bring them up to the same level.

The after-school sports activities in the Sections are closely supervised by educational agencies, and their work is regularly reviewed. The overall objectives of the Sections are to "assure the proper physical development of boys and girls of school age through sports; to develop in them, by means of sports, a socialist attitude toward effort, public property (sports equipment), self-discipline, good health habits, friendship (team spirit), and cooperation." High standards of sportsmanship—fair play, will to win, being a good loser and giving help to others who want to learn the game—are strongly encouraged.

Registration for membership in Sports Sections takes place once a year, in September. A child may join only one sport group. The Sections accept boys and girls who have passed the medical examination for physical education classes in their schools.

Training for all sports, in all Sections, begins with exercises and games that strengthen the body and tune up the muscles. Children must pass certain proficiency tests that will earn them an all-around athletic pin. The tests are on four levels. As he passes the test for each level, the child is given a specific rating. The highest is "Young Sportsman." The exercises that must be performed at each level are not easy. But they are important, for they get the body ready for successful training in a chosen sport.

When all the proficiency tests have been passed, work on the sport itself begins. The young sportsman then goes through a set pattern of training. A Skiing Section in a Pioneer Palace, for instance, would be set up in a definite way.

The children involved in the Section would be organized according to their age and previous experience. There would be separate groups for eleven to twelve, thirteen to fourteen, and fifteen to sixteen-year-olds. The youngest groups might have as many as 20 students, the next groups a maximum of 15, and the oldest not more than 10. This is because the training becomes more concentrated as the students advance in age.

The first and second age-groups meet twice a week for a two-hour session; the oldest, twice a week for a three- or four-hour session.

The youngest group spends 6 hours of the school year learning about the history of the sport of skiing, the development of the ski as a sport "tool," and the various types of ski shoes and poles used for the different forms of skiing. They also learn about the important use of skiing in World War II by the Red Army. They are taught proper health habits for skiers, the best diet for them, the benefits of swimming in toughening the skier.

The middle group spends 10 hours a year learning the development of the sport in the USSR. They discuss the

Students at a skiing school near Leningrad being trained from the start not to fear heights.

93

many special uses of skiing in war and in peacetime. They learn about famous Soviet skiers and analyze the techniques used by them. They are informed about the damage alcohol and smoking will do to a skier's physical fitness for his sport. They are instructed in giving first aid to a skier who is injured or suffers from frostbite. They are taught how to check on their own condition out on the slopes—to avoid strain, overexposure to the cold, falls and injuries.

The oldest group spends 14 hours a year studying about skiing and skiers on a far more advanced level.

The youngest group puts in 50 hours a year in acquiring greater physical stamina and relevant athletic skills—which they need to successfully practice the simpler techniques and tactics of skiing. The middle group puts in 42 hours in general and special physical exercises to prepare it for the training in techniques and tactics of more advanced forms of skiing. The oldest group spends 66 hours a year for a similar purpose, on a more advanced level. In the actual training for skill in various levels of technique and tactics, the three groups spend, in a year, 72 hours, 72 hours, and 108 hours, respectively.

A skiing trainee says: "I'm not a champion yet, I'm still learning."

Special exercises for future skiing champions at a skiing school.

Felix is a student at a skiing school. This is his first try at jumping.

Girl trainees at a skiing school setting off on a skiing hike.

Trainees in each group spend 6 hours a year in training to become assistant coaches to neighborhood skiing teams and school skiing clubs.

Every group spends a certain number of hours in competitions.

The total number of hours spent in training during the year is 144 hours for each of the two younger groups; 208 hours for the oldest.

To advance from one group to the next, the students have to pass rigorous tests.

The programs for Sports Sections that train young people in soccer, basketball, chess, skating, water sports, volleyball, and other sports follow the same general pattern.

When a young athlete in a Sports Section shows unusual talent but there is no Sports School to send him to in the area, he may be enrolled, with his own and his parents' approval, in a boarding school that does have such a Sports School. There is an increasing number of such boarding schools. There are also plans to establish boarding schools within walking distance of existing Sports Schools, so that the children need waste no time in getting to their sports sessions.

A Sports Section at a Regular School

School No. 4 in the town of Chekhov stands on a hill overlooking the Black Sea. This Crimean sea resort was named after the renowned Russian author, Anton Chekhov, who lived and wrote many of his works here. His plays and short stories are known wherever there is a theater or a library. He is read by all Russian children and teenagers, and many groups of schoolchildren come from Moscow to visit the town. Some of them even bring tents and stay a few days, in order to explore the surrounding countryside.

Some of the young visitors from the Soviet capital come not only to visit scenes related to Chekhov, however, but also to take part in The Moscow-Chekhov Matches. This annual sports competition is generally won by the children of Chekhov. The reason for this is that in School No. 4 nearly the entire student body is active in one or more sports. Many of the rooms have placards stating that everyone in the class belongs to a group in the school's Sports Section.

The school is known throughout the region for its winning teams. And the secret of their successes seems to lie in the large numbers of children who are seriously involved in sports. The school, here and in most of the USSR, does not concentrate on the few really gifted sportsmen, but seeks to train everyone, and in this way manages to develop a great many very good athletes. School No. 4 brims with sports talent. It has produced promising athletes in basketball, skiing, track and field, gymnastics, and in chess.

In fact, so well have the children of School No. 4 done in sports that a special Sports School has been established in the town of Chekhov. The students and their coaches made an appeal to the sports education authorities for the school, and their request was granted.

Those who do not attend the special school have not lost interest in sports. They compete as successfully as ever in local contests. And sports continue to be a central interest of all.

Committees of students take care of equipment. It seldom needs to be replaced. There is a group that takes care of repairing balls, skis, rackets, and skates. Another washes, irons, and mends jerseys and training shorts. Volodya Khrychev has developed into an expert mender of ski shoes, making old and beat-up ones look new again. There is no paid custodian to take care of the fields and courts. That, too, is done by a committee of students.

School No. 4 in the town of Chekhov is known all over the USSR, wherever children are interested in sports. The students' work in helping run the Sports Section and their high level of achievement are often praised in the youth press. And other schools strive to follow their example.

10

Backyards and Sandlots Teeming with Teams

IN THE IMMENSE AND SPRAWLING USSR, THERE ARE LARGE numbers of children for whom Sports Schools and Sports Sections are not yet available. They are the millions of children and teenagers who live in out-of-the-way towns, villages and hamlets, in newly started settlements, and in nomad sheepherding groups. Yet they, too, enjoy sports. And they, too, want to learn the proper techniques and test their abilities. It is assumed by sports leaders that among them there are many who possess the talents and the will-power to become outstanding Soviet sportsmen and sports-women.

These masses of youngsters are helped in an unusual way. The numerous newspapers and magazines published for school-age children offer the information they need about different sports and guide them in organizing teams and competitions.

There are twenty-eight such newspapers and thirty-two magazines. Together they reach 34 million young readers.

The most popular newspaper is the *Pionerskaya Pravda* (*Pioneer Truth*). The Moscow edition is the most important one but the paper is also published in twenty-eight different Soviet languages in many different cities, towns, and rural districts. It reaches some 15 million young readers. All schools and libraries subscribe to it, and it is hung prominently in every place where children gather.

Pionerskaya Pravda has been instrumental in organizing national sport clubs for members of backyard and sandlot teams. It tells how to find a coach, gives information about the rules of the games, prints notices of meets and matches, and gives suggestions for planning local and regional sports festivals. It even organizes national tournaments through a complicated system of announcements of matches placed in the paper.

The *Pionerskaya Pravda* also plays a strong part in organizing the *USSR School Games* (only the regular schools participate). The event draws in youngsters from all over the country. The matches start on the block or village level and advance to national finals. Participation in this event is especially encouraged in the rural and remote settlement areas. Teams from such places are allowed extra points.

The *USSR School Games* give coaches a chance to find special talent. When a young athlete has made a national team in the School Games, the local coach joins forces with a coach who has trained Olympic athletes. Together they undertake the student's future training. Such an athlete is also invited to all major competitive events to learn from observation and, from time to time, to participate. (Occasionally, an outstanding teenage athlete is allowed to compete in an international event. He is not expected to win, but to learn a lot from the experience.)

The paper's main efforts, however, are centered on setting up national sports clubs, which the backyard and sandlot teams can join for help in learning the sport and entering into competition.

The "Leather Ball" Soccer Club

Football (soccer) has the same fascination for most Soviet children as American football has for boys and girls in the United States. When a group, generally of boys, decides to organize a team, they will most likely apply to the paper for membership in the national "Leather Ball" Club. The team then receives the club's emblem, instructions on how to play and referee the game, information on how to tell a good coach from an inferior one and where to locate a coach, and guides as to how to go about contacting other teams for matches. When disputes occur at a game that the volunteer referee has not resolved to the satisfaction of the penalized team, it can write to the paper for a decision from a higher authority.

Lev Yashin, one of the greatest of Soviet football players, is the idol of sports-minded Soviet boys—which means pretty nearly *all* Soviet boys. Even at the height of his career, Lev Yashin found time to serve on the "Leather Ball" Club committee. He wrote frequently to young footballers in the pages of the Pioneer paper, as well as in other publications. In a jubilee edition of the Pioneer Handbook, he tells his fans about his own start in football and what it took to make it to the top:

"Which was my most exciting and rewarding game?" he begins,

The first one. It was during the War; I was fourteen, working in a munitions plant. It happened that the goalie of the plant team fell ill, and I was put in his place. That day I realized what sports means—that it isn't just goals. You don't just make points—you defend the honor of the plant in which you work. Or of your school or neighborhood. And when you put on the football jersey with the letters "CCCP" (USSR), you are expected to do honor to your country. Can people with weak nerves, without willpower, without guts, live up to the trust put in them by others? That is why I feel that the boys in the "Leather Ball" Club must first of all be loyal, courageous, and determined.

Then he went on to advise football enthusiasts on how to go about starting a team:

A team can be organized in any backyard, in any Pioneer group. Select the boys, apply to the *Pionerskaya* for membership, look up the Komsomols (Young Communist League members) in your community and ask one of them to be your coach, and you are all set. Only don't sulk when you don't win all the time. The shame is not in losing, it is in not trying hard enough. When boys ask me what it will take for the USSR team to win the world championship, I answer: "That you and your buddies practice more, become better players, deepen your desire to play well.

Like Yashin, other well-known Soviet football players also address their young fans with a genuine interest in seeing them do well.

"Leather Ball" teams all over the country play well. Every year a team from a *different* Soviet republic (there are fifteen in all) or Autonomous Region (there are twenty of these) leads in the *USSR School Games* football finals.

Boys from the age of thirteen play the adult form of the game. Younger ones play what is called "Mini-Football."

The Mini-Football "Leather Ball" Teams

This simplified form of football also requires the use of feet and head, and allows the use of hands only by the goalie. The players have to develop speed, strength, cunning in feinting, and lightning-quick reactions, sometimes even quicker ones than in the regular game.

Mini-football has been especially popular in Brazil, a world leader in the sport of football (soccer). Every living boy seems to play the mini game there. Soviet football teams have competed often with the Brazilians, and the Russian coaches now believe that the popularity of mini-football accounts for the excellence of their Brazilian rivals. So mini-football was introduced in the Soviet Union, and its popularity spread like wildfire. Even adult players began to like this form of the game.

Mini-football can be played almost anywhere—it does

Mini-soccer practice at a Tashkent, Uzbekistan, sports school.

not require a regulation size field. In the Soviet city of Baku, for instance, it is generally played on a tennis court. In mini-football the size of the team as well as the field are reduced. The playing time is shorter. The following table shows the variations possible:

| Size of Field (in meters) | Size of team, age of players, duration of game | |
	Ten–twelve years 40 minutes	Thirteen–fifteen years 50 minutes
15 × 30	4–5	4
20 × 40	5–6	5
25 × 50	6–7	5–6
30 × 60	7–8	6–7
35 × 63	8	7–8

The game is played in two halves with a 10-minute intermission. (The adult game, according to international rules, lasts for two 45-minute periods with a 10-minute intermission.)

The goals for mini-football are simple to make. Hockey goals may be used.

The rules are largely the same as for regular football, with some simplifications regarding the outside left and outside right positions and corner kicks.

Before the ball goes into action, each team stands on its own side of the field within a distance of 5 meters from the ball. The same distance is also maintained for free and penalty kicks. When the ball goes out of bounds, a member of the opposing team has the right to a free header. Penalty kicks are made from a mark 8 meters from the goal. Any number of substitutions may be made during the game, but only with players listed on the roster. There is only one referee and no assistants. The referee is usually an experienced teenage footballer.

The young boys are reminded as often as necessary that they are to play forcefully but not roughly, that they are to show consideration for their opponents, know how to lose

Puzzled why his mini-soccer team didn't win.

Mini-soccer practice in the snow is useful and is fun.

without bitterness or shame, obey the referee without argument, and honor all the rules.

To help mini-footballers become more skilled in their sport, the *Pioneer Magazine* has invented a game for its readers—"Number Football." It is played on a diagram with numbered squares printed in the magazine. The boys "move" the ball from one numbered square to another according to the rules of the game. The object is to find the best way of getting the ball into the goal. The readers are invited to send in their solutions. The magazine publishes the names of the ones who send in the best game plans.

Boys wearing the "Leather Ball" Club pin are admitted free to the major football matches. Most boys yearn to see at least one game between the two top national teams—*Dynamo* and *Spartak*. When they play against each other,

A trophy in the hands of the captain of the winning team in the finals of a national mini-soccer tournament.

the streets of Moscow seem deserted. "Everyone," you hear, "is today at the Luzhniki Stadium"—which seats 103,000, only a small fraction of the city's population of 6 million. Nevertheless, hundreds of boys wearing the pin manage to crowd into the Luzhniki to be spellbound by the perfect technique and dizzying speed of the fantastic footballers whom they hope to replace someday. And millions of their fellow "Leather Ball" club members, from the arctic North to the Azov Sea in the south, and from the Baltic in the west to the Pacific shores of the Soviet east, watch the game on television with almost equal excitement and hopes.

The "Golden Puck" Club

It is to be expected that ice hockey would be a popular sport in a country like the USSR, where winter lasts longer than any of the four seasons. The ground is covered with snow and the temperature is below freezing for several months at least in two-thirds of the country. When the weather is not right for football, the boys are ready for ice hockey.

To help all those who want to play but who have no training center nearby, the Pioneer paper organized the "Golden Puck" Club, in 1965.

The leader of this national movement to involve as many boys as possible in ice hockey is Anatoli Tarasov, head coach for the Red Army Hockey Society team. His team held the national championship in 1972, and surprised the West by nearly winning the world championship from the Canadian team in the same year. He is the head of the best known hockey school for young people.

The winners in an ice-hockey match of backyard teams.

Boys eleven to fifteen years of age may join a "Golden Puck" group. Separate teams are set up for eleven- to thirteen-year-olds and fourteen- to fifteen-year-olds. To qualify for membership, a player must help lay out his team's hockey rink and keep it in playing condition. To stay on the team after he has learned the game, he must help teach a group of younger boys in his vicinity how to play it. He must also get passing grades in school.

Equipment is provided by local factories, housing project managements, collective farm recreational groups, and various other organizations. To supply the growing Soviet population with adequate housing, millions of new apartments are built every year. The law requires that every new housing development must provide sports areas varying from small courts and playing fields (flooded for ice hockey) to gymnasiums and swimming pools.

The yearly "Golden Puck" national tournament is an exciting event for young hockey fans. The playoff for 1972 attracted about 3 million contestants.

In this tournament Tarasov spotted Sasha Frolov, a twelve-year-old Moscow schoolboy who played with remarkable skill. He invited Sasha to attend his school, where he would get the best training. Sasha is now one of the school's most promising hockey trainees.

One of the latest cities to join the "Golden Puck" movement is Tashkent, the capital of the Soviet republic of Uzbekistan—in Central Asia. Despite the warm climate of the city, comparable to that of the cotton-growing states in America, the city built a hockey stadium. The rink is covered with artificial ice. The first few teams that got together wrote to Moscow for hockey equipment, which was of course completely unavailable in a place with so mild a climate.

In most parts of the country, however, it is simple enough to procure hockey gear and to lay out rinks for the "Golden Puck" hockey hordes.

Sasha Tokarev, the best goalie among backyard teams competing for the "Golden Puck" prize.

The captain of the winning team at a city-wide ice-hockey meet holds up the "Golden Puck" trophy and is being held aloft in turn by his team's coach.

The winning team in the 7th annual National Ice-hockey Tournament for the "Golden Puck" prize (1971).

The "White Castle" Chess Club and
"Magic Checkers" Teams

Despite the fact that for many years chess has been a national passion with the Soviet people, *Pionerskaya Pravda* considers it important to help, through its pages, the large numbers of young enthusiasts who need encouragement and guidance to improve their game. In 1969, the paper began to organize a nationwide network of chess teams for boys and girls eleven to fifteen years of age. Together these teams make up the "White Castle" Club. In 1972 there were 25,000 such teams.

Using the militant terminology suggested by the game, the paper exhorts its young chess "recruits" to "take up arms" and "join the glorious battalions" of children whom "the number 64 entices to plan their own bold risks and winning moves on the battlefields of the chessboards." Team captains are summoned "to get ready for the decisive battle" in matches and tournaments, which the paper initiates. For the past several years, squadrons of quick-witted boys and girls have indeed "faced the storms and gales on the seas of this mental warfare."

The local teams, through competitions, select five of their best players—generally four boys and one girl. (This is the proportion of boys to girls among chess fans.) These players go to regional contests and the regional winners advance to national tournaments. The winning players are awarded "White Castle" medals and honorary prizes in the names of world chess champions.

As in other sports, Soviet chess champions work to attract boys and girls to the game. They tell them about their own trials and triumphs, share with them their expert knowledge.

For instance, Botvinnik—an ex-World Champion—writes in the newspaper for young people to explain that he has been using his scientific training to help perfect a chess-playing computer, which will be used to discover the thought patterns of chess players. This will help all chess players to anticipate the moves of a rival. Another champion, Tahl, writes in the paper: "I wonder which of you will be the champion of the year 2000!" Boris Spassky, the World Champion until he was beaten by Bobby Fischer (1972), says to the young chess lovers: "I am certain that those of you who today are chess fans will fight for the crown of world championship even before the year 2000!" And Nona Gaprindashvili, the world champion among women players, wrote, in 1972, urging girls to play: "Courage, girls! I wish you victory over the 'Kings' of your cocky male opponents. I hope that they will fall into your trap often."

The "Magic Checkers" Club movement was begun by the Pioneer paper much before the "White Castle" Club. The majority of the members are boys, but there is a larger minority of girls than in chess. The matches are played between selected teams of three boys and one girl, as compared with four boys and one girl for chess contests.

The champion Gorodetsky assures the young checker enthusiasts that the game is a "sport, an art, and a science." He warns that the checker expert must know how to read his opponent's mind and how to think up new and original attacks in the game.

There are about 450 Masters of Sports in checkers. The "Magic Checkers" Club for children has about one million members.

An Auto-Scooter Racers' Club

Boys and girls are encouraged to begin learning how a car works and how to drive one long before they reach the legal age for getting a driver's license. Those who want to get an early start, are invited to join an Auto-Scooter racing team and to become members of the national club for this sport run by the Pioneer newspaper. To become a member, the boy or girl writes to the paper for a pamphlet that gives instructions for making an auto-scooter and the rules for organizing races. After the applicant has built his scooter according to the specifications, he has to send in a photograph of it to the paper. If all is in order, a membership card is mailed to him.

Membership is open to boys and girls eleven to fifteen years of age. The leader of the team must be an adult to whom a driver's license has been issued, preferably an experienced chauffeur.

The would-be racers are urged to ask the managers of local factories and farm machinery supply centers for help with the materials and for the technical advice needed to assemble the motors for the scooters. Regional auto-supply centers have been directed to give out the small hubcaps, tires, and steering wheels required. (From time to time these miniature parts are shipped to the auto-supply depots for this purpose.)

With his membership card, the future motorist or racer

receives the Pioneer paper's good wishes: "Until we meet at the racetrack and on the highways of our country!"

The Auto-Scooter Club had 50,000 members in 1972.

Everyone on Skis

The Skiing Club movement for young people was started by the *Pionerskaya Pravda* in the early 1950s. The yearly skiing tournaments, held since the earliest days of the movement, have attracted more children and teenagers than any other sports contest arranged by the newspapers.

Soviet skiers have regularly been champions at international competitions. The children's ambitions are fired by the records scored by their countrymen and they work

A Soviet boy ski trainee carrying his skis marked "Made in Norway."

to improve their skiing skills with great concentration and enthusiasm.

In Russia, skiing has been a common way of traveling in winter for many years. It has also been important in hunting and in war. Most children learn how to ski at an early age. The members of the Skiing Club started by the Pioneer paper train in all forms of skiing, aided by the advice the paper gives.

Sledding and Coasting as a Sport

One of the newer sports in which Soviet people are showing a lively interest is sledding and coasting. The *Pionerskaya Pravda* has helped to increase its popularity among the children by printing information about it as an organized sport and giving specifications for building sleds and chutes.

Since the country is submerged in snow for so much of the year, the sled and the sledge have for centuries been put to practical uses—the sled for human transportation and the sledge for hauling goods. Now the sled serves as a vehicle for an exciting sport.

It is not uncommon now for a skilled sportsman to coast down a precipitous slope at the rate of 100 kilometers an hour. Moving at such a pace he enjoys the delightful sensation of flying without leaving the ground. He pushes off from the starting point, picks up momentum in a matter of seconds, and tears into a labyrinth of sharp turns and tricky curves. When the sled accidentally mounts the icy wall to the side of the chute, the athlete momentarily hangs there like a fly on a windowpane, until his quick thinking and strong leg and arm muscles get him out of the predicament and back onto the slick track. Leaning backward, with his legs stretched to the front end of the sled and touching ground, he lies almost flat to diminish the resistance of his head against the wind created by the speed of motion. Holding on to the reins in this difficult position, he maneuvers the sled down the steep slope and past the turns and curves.

Children start their training on coasting chutes, which are easy to make in a park, or on a nearby hill, or a sloping

A coasting chute in a public park in Moscow.

forest path. The recommended length for such a coasting chute is 200 to 300 meters; the width, 1.5 to 2 meters; the incline at the starting point must not be steeper than 70 degrees. For safety, a trestle is placed at the starting point as soon as a sled takes off. It is removed for the next sled only after the previous one has reached the end of the chute. This precaution prevents accidents, which could occur if more than one sled were on the track at the same time.

If there is an irremovable object along the slope, such as a large tree, a telephone pole, or a boulder, it is made less dangerous by being covered up to the necessary level with layers of sackcloth, straw, or piles of sawdust. The sides of the chute are lined with low walls made of wet earth that freezes to the hardness of ice in the winter. The chute is prepared in the autumn and is covered with pressed down snow or is flooded to form a smooth surface when winter sets in.

The technique of coasting for the beginning trainee is simple enough. He sits firmly in the very center of the sled; with one hand he grasps the reins (fastened to the front end); with the other he holds on firmly to the back end of the sled. He uses his feet for steering, resting them against the snow or ice of the chute. To maintain better balance, the beginner is advised to keep his feet parallel to the runners when making turns or going down curves.

After mastering the gentler slopes, the young sledder may test his skill on a chute used by accomplished sportsmen. These regulation chutes are 1,000 to 1,500 meters long and 1.4 to 1.6 meters wide. The inclines are very steep— 9 to 11 degrees. (These chutes are artificially made. They are first lined with tiles, wood, or concrete, then flooded to form an ice surface as smooth as glass.)

The regulation sled used in Soviet sport coasting is not a toboggan.* It is smaller and narrower. One type seats a single person; another two people. The sleds have relatively high runners (metal), which are set 45 centimeters apart and are knife-edge sharp. A fraction of a second may decide the winning score. Therefore a nick on the edge of the runner may make the difference between winning and losing a contest.

Coasting enthusiasts work out even in warm seasons—in specially designed carts. Riding and maneuvering such a cart strengthens neck and arm muscles. Young sledders also exercise with dumbbells for the same purpose.

Sledding and coasting is one more winter sport to help young people turn the frigid Russian winter into a season of many pleasures.

The "Winged Ball" Club

It was American firemen who invented volleyball. Between fire alarms, they would string a rope across two poles and play the first, simple version of the game. It was a way of battling boredom between fires. The popularity of volleyball has spread throughout the world. In Soviet Russia, countless boys and girls enjoy the sport. There are not enough Sports Schools and Sports Sections where volleyball is taught, so the Pioneer newspaper set out to help young

---

* A toboggan is a long sled, seating as many as five persons; it usually has no runners. It is made of thin boards curved back at the front end; it often has side rails.

Volleyball practice at a sports school on a state farm (kolkhoz) *near Moscow.*

volleyball fans learn the game and compete in it in an organized way. For this purpose it set up a system of teams, all part of the "Winged Ball" Club.

This is one team sport in which Soviet girls participate as much as boys. Volleyball is especially popular in the warmer parts of the country—the Ukraine, the Crimea, and the Central Asian areas, where the game can be played outdoors much of the year.

Basketball Clubs

Basketball coaches in the USSR lay special stress on exercises to strengthen the left arm and hand. Basketball players must be able to use both arms and hands equally well. This is emphasized repeatedly in the Pioneer paper, which has started a sort of junior basketball league all over the country.

In a recent issue a leading coach is quoted as saying: "Soviet basketball today, is actually a melting pot of different styles typical of players from various Soviet republics. The style of the national team blends Russian athleticism (power, speed), Baltic—Latvian, Lithuanian, Estonian—rationality (the cool and calculated approach), Georgian (Georgia is in the Caucasus) improvisation (surprise moves)." This mixture of styles has evidently not been a drawback. The 1972 Olympic Games team that won in Munich had players from all these parts of the USSR.

Young basketball players and their coach at a basketball school in Latvia.

At a children's basketball school in Latvia. A friendly match.

Basketball is very popular with Moscow children.

An exciting basketball match in a national tournament—the rivals are girls from the Ukraine and the Russian Federation.

With thousands of junior basketball teams in every corner of the country, it is to be expected that in the future the "melting pot" will continue to offer stiff competition to the best foreign teams. There are 3.5 million registered basketball players in the country, three-fourths of them primary and secondary school students.

Speed and Figure Ice-Skating

The long cold winters, the wide open spaces of the Russian *steppe* (plains), and the rivers and lakes with which the country abounds, provide excellent conditions for ice-skating. Come winter, those children who are not on skis or sleds have their winter fun on skates. It is easy to visualize nearly all Russian youngsters turning the harsh winter into a season of many delights as they skitter about on their skis or sleds or skates.

Four-time Olympic champion, speed skater E. Grishin, was invited to write a piece for the *Pionerskaya Pravda,* giving some pointers to beginners in the paper's Skating Club. He wrote an article advising the *novichki* (beginners) to begin their training on "Snowmaidens"—as beginners' skates are called—then to advance to hockey skates but *not* to "Canadians" (special skates worn by speedy adult skaters); and only when they became quite skilled to start using speed skates. He then instructed them in how best to lace their skating shoes, what movements to practice and in what order, how to coordinate the position of the shoulders with the movement of the legs. He pointed out that in speed skating the arms work in the same way as in running. The children were urged not to be discouraged if they could not skate on a large rink, for, he assured them, "the road to championship began for some speed skaters on a frozen fishing pond or a flooded football field."

Writing for young people is not the only way famous athletes help popularize sports among Soviet children. They are also present at tournaments, where they personally hand the prizes to the winners and praise the rest for their fine efforts. This contact with accomplished athletes makes young people feel that they are a real part of the Soviet sports world.

The Pioneer press has invented three games to help speed skaters improve their skill; the games are described in the jubilee issue of the Pioneer Handbook.

Students at a sports school for figure skating in a suburb of Moscow.

Pistol: A number of skaters line up behind one another, each holding on to the waist of the one in front. When the column has started to move and worked up speed, the leader commands everyone to squat and extend the right or left leg (a typical Russian folk dancing position). The trick is not to lose balance, to return to the upright position still holding on to the one ahead, and to skate on until the next order is given by the leader.

Under the Bridge: The skaters choose two leaders who then hold hands, raise their arms and stand 1 meter apart. The rest attempt to skate under this "bridge" without touching either one of the leaders with their backs or heads. The game continues until only three or four players have not been eliminated. Then a new "bridge" is chosen and the game goes on.

Through the Open Gate: Several hurdles are placed opposite each other on a skating rink. A wooden board is laid across each pair of hurdles, first at a height of 1 meter. The skaters approach with speed and try to skate under the "gate" without knocking it down. Those who are not eliminated try again with the board placed lower. The winner is the one who skates under the lowest "gate." The game may be made more difficult by having the players skate under the opening on only one leg.

There is also a countrywide movement to teach figure skating to masses of children. *The Pionerskaya Pravda* and the figure skating schools are encouraging this. In Moscow, for instance, there are posters at every skating rink inviting children and teenagers to enroll for free instruction and practice. To give balance to the program, these figure skating centers offer calisthenics, elements of music appreciation, and ballet dancing. All of these are needed to achieve the endurance, muscle control and grace of movement needed for fine figure skating.

Marina Savaya began her training in one of these centers. When she was thirteen, she participated in the world championship competition in Calgary, Canada. "So far," reported a Soviet sports journalist with a touch of humor, "her biggest reward has been a kiss and big hug from her parents, but she skated with champions Karen Magnussen and Janet Lynn."

The traditional ten-day Winter Holidays are celebrated with the characteristic Russian flair for colorful ceremonies and festivals. One of the typical features is exhibition figure skating, and large numbers of children take part. Children who come to watch often decide that they, too, would like to learn to skate well. And so the number of young skaters grows.

The program of the Figure Skating Club, the enthusiasm with which champion skaters inspire the young, the Winter Holidays, and the general availability of rinks and coaching —both free of charge—have made figure skating a favorite pastime for the vast numbers of boys and girls.

Speed-skating trainees on a 200-meter run.

Figure skaters train on an artificial ice rink at a sports school in Kazakhstan, a Soviet republic in southeastern Asia. The area has a moderate climate.

Girls at a sports school for figure skating in Moscow perform a folk dance.

Between 9 and 10 million children and teenagers took part in the 1971 national competitions in track and field events. Most of them were young people who had been organized into backyard, block, village, and other small-scale community teams through the initiative of the Pioneer press. Because good fellowship is a part of good competitive sports, the paper decided to organize track and field teams into a national Friendship Club.

Members of these far-flung groups are closely observed at regional and national track and field competitions, and the good ones are singled out for more intensive training. They are helped to attend a special sports school or Sports Section for track and field athletics.

The great popularity of this sport has created a need for thousands of coaches. In 1972 there were 42,000 track and field coaches in the USSR.

Children going into track and field sports must start by earning the GTO pin. The three letters in "GTO" stand for the Russian words meaning *Prepared* for *Labor* and *Self-Defense*. To wear the GTO pin, the young person has to pass tests that show he is fit for hard work at school or on a job and for self-defense in case of war. The tests that children have to pass to earn the pin consist mostly of track- and field-type exercises.

Recently a program has been started to encourage all children to try for the GTO pin. This may account for the astronomical number of youngsters in the track and field Friendship Club.

*Three-time European champion sprinter—800 meters—Evegenii
Arzhanov (1972).*

A Correspondence Sports School

The children's magazine, *Koster* (*Campfire*), conducts in a special section of the magazine, a kind of correspondence school for children in remote areas. It knows that there are still in the USSR many thousands of square miles of sparsely populated areas—distant villages, hamlets, new settlements. Facilities for sports in such cut-off communities are very scarce. Yet the children there are also in need of the benefits and fun of competitive sports. Eventually such communities will have sports centers for their young people, but in the meantime, the magazine *Koster* tries to help. Each month it carries training exercises, instruction for making equipment and laying out playing fields. One issue even suggested a practical way of rigging up an outdoor shower with a bucket, a piece of pipe, a piece of rope, and a foot pedal.

The magazine prints quizzes regularly, asking the readers to send in their answers. Any child may write to the sports editor for additional information and guidance in solving special problems.

From time to time, the magazine selects children from these areas, by mail, and finances their way to summer camps where they can compete with children who have had direct rather than correspondence-course training in sports. The organizers of the *Koster* Correspondence Sports School told me that they were amazed at how well their "students" performed in contests at camp. These long-distance trainees proved that where there is a will to enjoy sports, even a magazine can show the way.

Koster sports editors are particularly proud of their

School for Runners—*Shkola Sprynt* they call it. All a child needs to do to enroll is send in his name, age, and address. For the past eight years, *Koster* has carefully presented in its pages a full course of training for running various distances. The "lessons" are cleverly illustrated.

The correspondence-school section of the magazine was originated by two imaginative young men—one a sports photographer and graduate from a Physical Education Institute, the other a strong sports fan and children's author.

11

Summing Up

IT WOULD BE INCORRECT TO ASSUME THAT THE DIVERSE, IN-
tensive, and costly Soviet sports program for children and
youth is meant to serve mainly one purpose—that of training world champions.

This is unquestionably one of the important aims—but
only one of several. Training in sports is wholeheartedly
supported by the Government, by educational authorities,
and the public because they all see it as providing for the
young sports lover a road to good health, stamina, good
attitudes toward effort and achievement, good feelings about
himself, his team, and his rivals—and, not least, good fun.

The Leningrad coach who said, "A diamond becomes
a diamond only after the jeweler has worked on it" expressed the thoughts of all conscientious Soviet educators.
Helping boys and girls enjoy sports is just one way to
achieve this purpose.

In the USSR, the seriousness with which young people are trained in sports is not unlike the way other children there are trained to become excellent musicians or dancers. There is the same typical striving for perfection. And from all evidence, the young people themselves are willing to train long and hard despite the years of work and the disappointments and occasional discouragement that are mingled with the satisfactions and the fun.

On the basis of my own observations, the young sports enthusiasts, many of whom are pictured in this book, are not only physically sound but have a buoyancy and vitality that can be attributed to their sports activities. Those I saw certainly worked hard but liked what they were doing. Though the program is demanding, it has for them its lighter aspects. The strain is eased by the excitement and ritual of sporting events, the affection for the devoted coach, the journeys to competitions, and the thrill of sometimes being a hero. The sports star is seen not as a superman but as a superior human being. Another compensation to the excelling young athlete is the opportunity to travel to African, Asian, and other third-world countries, to help train young sportsmen there. Quite a number of graduates from sports schools are selected for this purpose.

At the same time, not every talented young athlete is determined to become a star. I witnessed the following scene at a Sports Section gymnasium to which a coach from the USSR Gymnastic Federation had come in search of champion material. The elegantly dressed visitor, his lapel bedecked with an impressive number of athletic pins, approached the flushed Mitya, who had just finished a number of very difficult stunts on the rings. Mitya was fourteen.

"Well, young man, I have good news for you. You no longer need to worry about your future. I'll undertake your training myself."

"But I haven't been worrying about it," said Mitya. "Thanks for your offer—only I'm already giving as much time to sports as I can spare. I can't afford anymore."

"Look, don't you realize that I'll make you a world champion?" the visitor said heatedly.

"I admit that that's possible," the boy replied calmly, "but it's not what I want to do with my life."

As the visiting coach turned on his heel, I saw Mitya's regular coach, whom the youngsters affectionately called "Uncle Kolya," smile and nod his head in approval.

The matter of sports involving the many national groups of the Soviet Union is an interesting one. In order to make it possible for members of the many smaller nationalities to take part in countrywide and international events, children in these areas are encouraged to concentrate on the sports that are popular in most of the world and in the larger part of their own country. The native sports—special types of wrestling, reindeer and dogsled racing, local forms of horsemanship—are learned, however, and can be seen at local folk festivals and in seasonal holiday celebrations. Over a million people, young and old, participate in such sports events. However, although these people care about their native sports, they want, above all, to be part of the wider sports world—especially the children. (Just the same, they remain proud of their ethnic origins, as was demonstrated when a USSR tennis star, taking part

Uzbek boys of Uzbekistan, Soviet Central Asia, engaged in a local form of wrestling called **Kurash**.

A reindeer race on the island of Sakhalin in the Soviet Pacific northwest.

Teenage Uzbek horsewoman and her racer.

in an international tournament, complained because re-porters referred to him as a "Russian" when he was actually Georgian.)

All this is not to say that in so broad a program, involving so many institutions, organizations, and individuals, things do not go wrong from time to time. Some coaches become too ambitious and exert too much influence and pressure on their young trainees. Some of the young people lose perspective and neglect their studies. Now and then a young ex-world champion finds it extremely upsetting to have to take up a more ordinary life. A few overeager athletes for-get that "It's not whether you win or lose but how you play the game that counts." When uncovered, these failings come in for strong criticism. Yet they do exist, as they do in all sports-minded countries.

Generally, however, there is a determined effort to use the sports program to build character as well as bodies. Winning is important, as it is everywhere, but for every winner there have to be losers, and learning how to lose without becoming demoralized is also stressed. As one So-viet sports leader put it: "Victories and defeats—both are beneficial. They both steel the individual, test his willpower and his confidence in himself." Ernest Hemingway, an American author who is widely read and admired in the Soviet Union, and whose association with sports is appreci-ated by young Soviet athletes, expressed the same thought as follows: "Sports teach you to win honestly. Sports teach you to lose with dignity. Thus, sports teach everything—they teach life . . . ." Many Soviet athletes know these words, and recognize their truth.

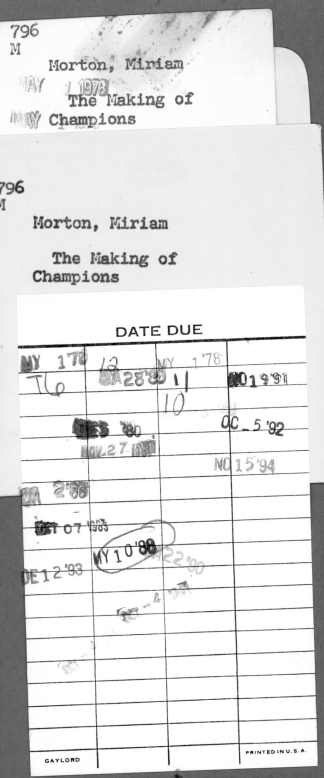

796
M

Morton, Miriam

The Making of
Champions

796
M

Morton, Miriam

The Making of
Champions

DATE DUE

MY 1 '78		MY 1 '78	
T6	JA 28 '89		NO 19 '91
		10	
	DES '80		OC 5 '92
	NOV 27		NO 15 '94
JA 2 '86			
OCT 07 1983			
DE 12 '93	MY 10 '88	JA 22 '00	

GAYLORD   PRINTED IN U.S.A.